Sewing by Heart

Sewing by Heart

Tone Finnanger

Tilda®

www.tildasworld.com

CONTENTS

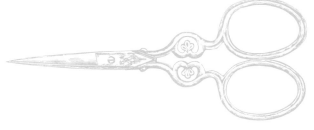

INTRODUCTION

Fabric design has become a passion for me and it's just wonderful to see a graphic artwork becoming a lovely fabric print that you can turn into so many beautiful items. For this book, I wanted to create patchwork, appliqué and quilting projects that combined several Tilda fabric collections in one book. Few things are more joyful than playing with colours and patterns and trying out different compositions and shapes, and this book is all about the love of fabric and creating what is in your heart.

Tilda Sewing by Heart contains a wide range of projects, both large and small, that will take you through every season, beginning with a Bumblebee Quilt for spring and ending with a cozy Patchwork Stocking for winter. The book is packed with quilts, pillows and softies, all in bright, happy colours and patterns. We used five different Tilda collections – Cabbage Rose released in autumn 2016, the spring and summer 2017 Bumblebee and Circus collections and the brand-new autumn and winter 2017 Harvest and Cottage collections. Details of the fabrics used have been given in the projects but if you can't get hold of every fabric, there are plenty of other fabrics in similar colours that you can easily replace them with. I hope you will find projects that inspire you.

There is a dedicated team behind this book. I design the products and ideas and work closely with Ingun Eldøy, who does all the sewing, and Linda Clements who writes the explanations and does most of the illustrations. I am so grateful for their talents and would not be able to develop this book without them. I have also had amazing help from stylists Line Dammen and Ingrid Skaansar, photographers Inger Marie Grini and Sølvi Dos Santos, and graphic designers Anna Wade and Prudence Rogers. A big thank you also goes to my publisher Ame Verso and F&W Media International for all their great support.

Very best regards

BUMBLEBEE QUILT

This pretty quilt uses gentle curves to make units that once joined together create a lovely hour-glass pattern waving serenely down the quilt. The quilt has forty blocks, all made in the same way with a template. It uses fabrics from the gorgeous Bumblebee collection.

Finished Size 55in x 73in (140cm x 185.5cm)

FIG A
Fabric swatches
If you can't get hold of one or more of these fabrics, just replace with fabrics in similar colours

Fabric 1
Solid
off-white

Fabric 2
Sunny Park
ginger

Fabric 3
Cherry
Blossom teal

Fabric 4
Flower Nest
ginger

Fabric 5
Rosa Mollis
teal

Fabric 6
Garden Bees
ginger

Fabric 7
Rosa Mollis
green

Fabric 8
Flower Nest
teal

Fabric 9
Garden Bees
green

Fabric 10
Flower Nest
green

Fabric 11
Sunny Park
green

Fabric 12
Flower Nest
pink

Fabric 13
Rosa Mollis
linen

Fabric 14
Sunny Park
pink

Fabric 15
Cherry Blossom
pink

Fabric 16
Garden Bees
pink

Fabric 17
Garden Bees
blue

Fabric 18
Sunny Park
golden

Fabric 19
Cherry Blossom
blue

Fabric 20
Rosa Mollis
golden

Fabric 21
Flower Nest
blue

MATERIALS

- Fabric 1: 1¾yd (1.5m) – Solid off-white
- Fabric 2: ¼yd (25cm) – Sunny Park ginger
- Fabric 3: ⅜yd (40cm) – Cherry Blossom teal
- Fabric 4: ¼yd (25cm) – Flower Nest ginger
- Fabric 5: ¼yd (25cm) – Rosa Mollis teal
- Fabric 6: ¼yd (25cm) – Garden Bees ginger
- Fabric 7: ⅜yd (40cm) – Rosa Mollis green
- Fabric 8: ⅜yd (40cm) – Flower Nest teal
- Fabric 9: ⅜yd (40cm) – Garden Bees green
- Fabric 10: ⅜yd (40cm) – Flower Nest green
- Fabric 11: ⅜yd (40cm) – Sunny Park green
- Fabric 12: ⅜yd (40cm) – Flower Nest pink
- Fabric 13: ½yd (50cm) – Rosa Mollis linen
- Fabric 14: ⅜yd (40cm) – Sunny Park pink
- Fabric 15: ½yd (50cm) – Cherry Blossom pink
- Fabric 16: ⅜yd (40cm) – Garden Bees pink
- Fabric 17: ¼yd (25cm) – Garden Bees blue
- Fabric 18: ¼yd (25cm) – Sunny Park golden
- Fabric 19: ⅜yd (40cm) – Cherry Blossom blue
- Fabric 20: ¼yd (25cm) – Rosa Mollis golden
- Fabric 21: ¼yd (25cm) – Flower Nest blue
- Backing fabric 3½yd (3.25m) of standard width
- Wadding (batting) 63in x 81in (160cm x 206cm)
- Binding fabric ½yd (50cm) – Solid off-white
- Template plastic or thin card to make template

Preparation and Cutting Out

1 Before you start, refer to General Techniques: Making Quilts and Pillows. There are forty blocks in the quilt in a 5 x 8 block layout. Each block is made up of four quarters, with each made from two curved shapes, sewn in the same way from a template. A border of rectangles is added at the top and bottom of the quilt. The fabrics used for the quilt are shown in **Fig A** and the quilt layout in **Fig B**.

FIG B

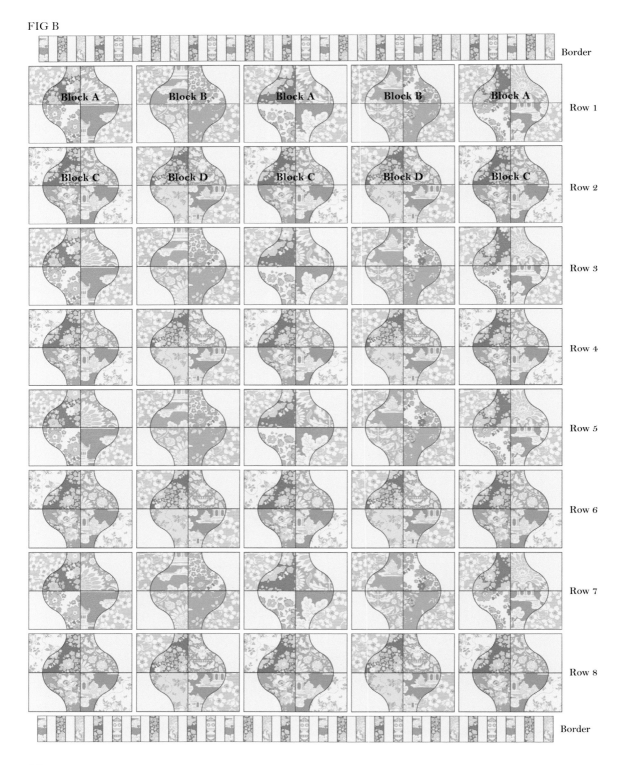

2 Use template plastic or thin card to create a template, using the pattern provided (see Patterns section). Each block is made up of eight pieces, some rotated to create the vertical curving pattern. All of these are cut from the same template but for four of the shapes the template shape is reversed. The easiest way to do this when cutting out the shapes is to use the template on the *right* side (RS) of the fabric for four of the shapes and on the *wrong* side (WS) of the fabric for the other four shapes. **Fig C** shows this, with Cutting Method RS and Cutting Method WS. The most economical use of the fabric is achieved by following this diagram, and you should be able to cut eleven shapes along a 5in (12.7cm) x width of fabric strip. The strips are cut at 5in (12.7cm) deep, which is a little deeper than the height of the template. **Fig D** shows the orientation of the eight shapes for one block, with the cutting methods used. When cutting out the shapes from each fabric take *great care* to check **Fig B** for *each* block, which shows all of the fabrics and the way that the pieces need to be cut so the curves appear the correct way.

FIG C
Cutting Method RS – fabric right *side up*

Cutting Method WS – fabric wrong *side up*

FIG D

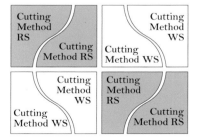

3 From Fabric 1 cut the following.
* Eight 5in (12.7cm) x width of fabric strips. Sub-cut into eighty template shapes for the blocks, in the orientations shown in **Fig B**. Refer to this diagram for all the fabric cutting.
* Four 1½in (3.8cm) x width of fabric strips. Sub-cut fifty-four 1½in x 3in (3.8cm x 7.6cm) rectangles, for the borders.

4 Cut the following numbers of template shapes from 5in (12.7cm) x width of fabric strips.
* Fabric 2 – one strip for eight shapes.
* Fabric 3 – two strips for sixteen shapes.
* Fabric 5 – one strip for eight shapes.
* Fabric 7 – two strips for twelve shapes.
* Fabric 8 – two strips for twelve shapes.
* Fabric 9 – two strips for twelve shapes.
* Fabric 10 – two strips for twelve shapes.
* Fabric 11 – two strips for twelve shapes.
* Fabric 13 – three strips for twenty-four shapes.
* Fabric 15 – three strips for twenty-four shapes.
* Fabric 17 – one strip for eight shapes.
* Fabric 18 – one strip for eight shapes.
* Fabric 19 – two strips for sixteen shapes.
* Fabric 20 – one strip for eight shapes.
* Fabric 21 – one strip for eight shapes.

5 From Fabric 4 cut the following.
* One 5in (12.7cm) x width of fabric strip. Sub-cut eight template shapes.
* One 1½in (3.8cm) x width of fabric strip. Sub-cut twelve 1½in x 3in (3.8cm x 7.6cm) rectangles.

6 From Fabric 6 cut the following.
* One 5in (12.7cm) x width of fabric strip. Sub-cut eight template shapes.
* One 1½in (3.8cm) x width of fabric strip. Sub-cut ten 1½in x 3in (3.8cm x 7.6cm) rectangles.

7 From Fabric 12 cut the following.
* Two 5in (12.7cm) x width of fabric strips. Sub-cut twelve template shapes.
* One 1½in (3.8cm) x width of fabric strip. Sub-cut ten 1½in x 3in (3.8cm x 7.6cm) rectangles.

8 From Fabric 14 cut the following.
- Two 5in (12.7cm) x width of fabric strips. Sub-cut twelve template shapes.
- One 1½in (3.8cm) x width of fabric strip. Sub-cut twelve 1½in x 3in (3.8cm x 7.6cm) rectangles.

9 From Fabric 16 cut the following.
- Two 5in (12.7cm) x width of fabric strips. Sub-cut twelve template shapes.
- One 1½in (3.8cm) x width of fabric strip. Sub-cut twelve 1½in x 3in (3.8cm x 7.6cm) rectangles.

10 From the binding fabric cut seven 2½in (6.4cm) x width of fabric strips. Sew the strips together end to end and press seams open. Press the binding in half along the length, wrong sides together.

Making a Block

11 There are forty blocks in the quilt, all made in the same way. The blocks are assembled in rows, with the fabric order repeating, so Rows 1, 3, 5 and 7 use the same fabrics and Rows 2, 4, 6 and 8 use the same fabrics. Make one block as follows. Refer to **Fig B** and start by selecting the correct fabric shapes for the first block (top row, far left on the diagram) – Fabrics 15, 12, 16, 1, 8, 1, 14 and 15. Lay out the pieces to check that they are the correct orientations (see **Fig E**).

FIG E

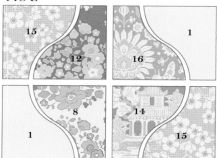

12 Take two curved pieces and carefully pin them right sides together along their curved edges. **Fig F** shows a Fabric 1 piece and a Fabric 16 piece. Use as many pins as needed to match the edges exactly. Now sew the shapes together using a ¼in (6mm) seam allowance. Sew slowly and follow the curve accurately. Press the seam to one side. Repeat this process to sew the other units of the block into curved pairs (**Fig G**). Sew two units together for each half of the block. Now sew the two halves of the block together, matching the centre seam carefully. Press the block and check that it is 11½in x 9in (29.2cm x 22.9cm).

FIG F

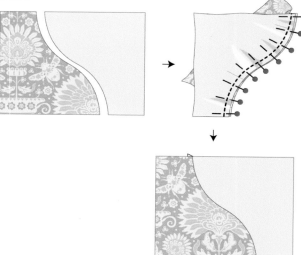

FIG G

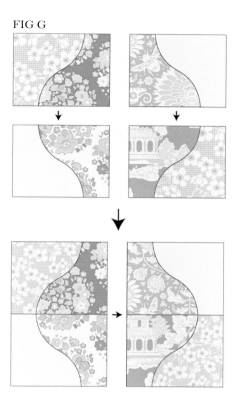

13 Repeat to make the rest of the blocks, working your way across the rows and checking carefully each time that the fabrics and the curved shapes are correct before you sew them together. **Fig H** shows that there are four different blocks in the quilt. This fabric order repeats in a regular pattern.

FIG H

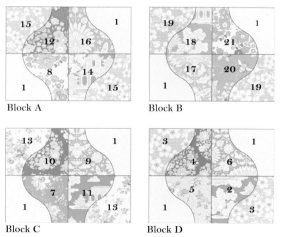

Block A

Block B

Block C

Block D

Making the Borders

14 The border uses a repeating pattern of rectangles of Fabrics 14, 4, 16, 12 and 6, with Fabric 1 rectangles in between (**Fig I**). Each border has fifty-five rectangles in total: twenty-seven in off-white and twenty-eight in prints. Lay out the pieces in the correct order for the top border. Sew the rectangles together along the long sides and press seams to one side, or open. Each border should measure 55½in (141cm) long. Repeat to make the bottom border.

FIG I

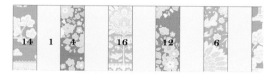

14   1   4   16   12   6

Assembling the Quilt

15 Lay out the blocks in the order shown in **Fig B**. Sew them together row by row. Press the seams in alternate rows in opposite directions. Now sew the rows together, matching seams neatly. Press long seams open or to one side. Finally, sew the top and bottom borders in place and press. The borders should fit the horizontal measurement of the quilt but ease to fit if need be.

Quilting and Finishing

16 Cut the backing fabric across the width into two equal pieces. Sew together along the long side and press the seam open. Trim to a piece about 64in x 82in (162.5cm x 208.3cm). Make a quilt sandwich of the backing fabric, wadding (batting) and quilt. Quilt as desired. Square up the quilt, trimming excess wadding and backing.

17 Use the prepared binding to bind your quilt – see General Techniques: Binding. Add a label to your lovely quilt to finish.

BUMBLEBEE PILLOWS

*Inspired by the Bumblebee Quilt, these two pillows feature blocks from the quilt and use some of the same fabrics, so refer to the fabric swatches in **Fig A** of the quilt. Instructions and materials are given for the long pillow. The short pillow (overleaf) uses the same techniques but different fabrics and fewer blocks. Note that instead of solid off-white, the long pillow uses solid ginger and solid pink, while the short pillow uses solid olive and solid teal.*

Finished Sizes
Long pillow: 44in x 17in (111.8cm x 43.2cm)
Short pillow: 22in x 17in (56cm x 43.2cm)

MATERIALS

Long Bumblebee Pillow
- Fabric 1A: 5in (12.7cm) x width of fabric strip – Solid ginger
- Fabric 1B: 5in (12.7cm) x width of fabric strip – Solid pink
- Two print fabrics, eight 5in (12.7cm) squares of each (see Step 3)
- Eight print fabrics, four 5in (12.7cm) squares of each (see Step 3)
- Wadding (batting) 46in x 19in (116.8cm x 48.3cm)
- Lining fabric 46in x 19in (116.8cm x 48.3cm) (optional)
- Fabric for back of cushion, two pieces 26in x 17½in (66cm x 44.5cm)
- Binding fabric ⅜yd (40cm) – Flower Nest teal
- Three ¾in (2cm) buttons for pillow back

LONG BUMBLEBEE PILLOW

1 From Fabric 1A (solid ginger) use the Bumblebee Quilt template to cut eight shapes from the 5in (12.7cm) x width of fabric strip.

2 From Fabric 1B (solid pink) use the Bumblebee Quilt template to cut eight shapes from the 5in (12.7cm) x width of fabric strip.

3 From the ten print fabrics, cut the following pieces using the template.
- Eight each from Fabric 3 and Fabric 15.
- Four each from Fabric 4, 6, 5, 2, 12, 16, 8 and 14.

4 From the binding fabric cut four 2½in (6.4cm) x width of fabric strips. Sew together and prepare as a double-fold binding.

5 To make the long pillow, follow the Bumblebee Quilt instructions to make the blocks, making four of Block A and four of Block D. Note that instead of solid off-white, Block A uses solid ginger and Block D uses solid pink. **Fig A** here shows the blocks.

FIG A

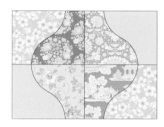

Block A   Block D

6 Place the eight blocks in the alternating order shown in **Fig B** here. Sew them together in rows and then sew the rows together.

FIG B

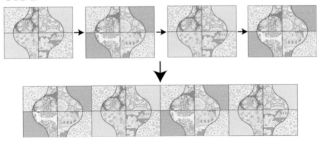

7 Make a quilt sandwich of the patchwork, wadding (batting) and lining fabric (if using). Quilt as desired.

8 The pillow is assembled with an overlapped back, with buttons to secure. Use the two pieces of back fabric and follow the instructions in General Techniques: Button-Fastening Cushion. To finish, use the prepared binding to bind the cushion edge (see General Techniques: Binding).

SHORT BUMBLEBEE PILLOW

This pillow uses just four blocks from the Bumblebee Quilt – two of Block B and two of Block C. Instead of solid off-white it uses solid olive and solid teal and ten green/blue print fabrics. Follow **Fig C** here for the blocks and **Fig D** here for the pillow assembly. Once pieced, the patchwork is 22½in x 17½in (57.1cm x 44.5cm). Make a quilt sandwich and quilt as desired. Make up the cushion in the same way as the Long Bumblebee Pillow, using fabric pieces suitable for the size of this pillow. For the binding use three 2½in (6.4cm) x width of fabric strips from Flower Nest blue.

FIG D

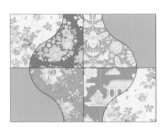

FIG C

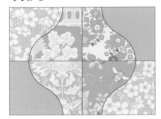

Block B

Block C

BEE APPLIQUÉ PILLOW

Practise your appliqué with this lovely pillow. A technique using paper patterns has been used, in the same way as the Cabbage Rose Quilt, created from the shapes given in the Patterns section.

Finished Size 22in x 13in (56cm x 33cm)

FIG A
Fabric swatches
If you can't get hold of one or more of these fabrics, just replace with fabrics in similar colours

Fabric 1
Solid
off-white

Fabric 8
Flower Nest
teal

Fabric 2
Solid
teal

Fabric 9
Garden Bees
pink

Fabric 3
Solid
olive

Fabric 10
Flower Nest
ginger

Fabric 4
Solid
pink

Fabric 11
Garden Bees
ginger

Fabric 5
Solid
ginger

Fabric 12
Flower Nest
green

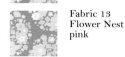

Fabric 6
Cherry
Blossom teal

Fabric 13
Flower Nest
pink

Fabric 7
Cherry
Blossom blue

MATERIALS
- Fabric 1: 1yd (1m) – Solid off-white
- Scraps (about 5in/12.7cm square) of four solid fabrics and eight print fabrics – see **Fig A** for the actual fabrics used
- Wadding (batting) 23in x 14in (58.4cm x 35.5cm)
- Binding fabric ¼yd (25cm) – Flower Nest pink
- Thick coated paper for paper piece appliqués
- Paper piece glue
- Sharp, pointed scissors
- Pointy stick and tweezers (optional)

Making the Pillow

1 The fabrics used are shown in **Fig A** but you could use your own fabric choices if you prefer. A charm pack could also be used. See **Fig B** for the pillow layout.

2 Cut Fabric 1 as follows.
- One piece 23in x 14in (58.4cm x 35.5cm) for the appliqué background.
- One piece 23in x 14in (58.4cm x 35.5cm) for backing when quilting.
- Two pieces 16in x 13½in (40.6cm x 34.3cm) for the back of pillow cover.

3 From the binding fabric cut two 2½in (6.4cm) x width of fabric strips.

4 Fold the Fabric 1 appliqué background 23in x 14in (58.4cm x 35.5cm) piece into quarters to lightly crease the halfway points. This will help you position the appliqués. The background is cut slightly larger to allow frayed edges to be trimmed later.

5 Copy the pattern shapes onto thick coated paper and cut out using sharp, pointed scissors. The basic process is described here – for more detail see the Cabbage Rose Quilt: Making the Appliqué Blocks. Cut out a fabric shape ¼in (6mm) larger all round than the paper shape (**Fig C**). Snip notches in the edge of the fabric. Spread glue along the edge of the paper and fold the seam allowance over the shape (**Fig D**). Work all round the shape and press. Prepare all shapes this way.

FIG C   FIG D

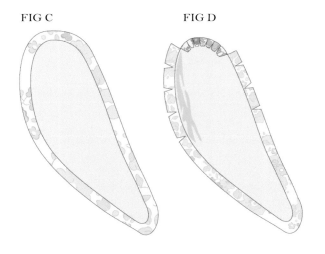

6 To prepare the stems, cut fabric strips about 6in (15.2cm) long x ⅜in (1cm) wide, in the fabrics shown in **Fig B**. Spread glue over the wrong side of a strip and fold the edges in towards the middle. The strips can be trimmed to the correct lengths when you begin to position the flowers.

7 Place the prepared appliqués on the background as shown in **Fig B**. Cut the stems to the lengths needed and position under the flowers, so raw ends are covered. Use a little glue to stick the pieces to the background fabric, or use pins or tacking (basting) stitches. Sew the appliqués to the background fabric with tiny invisible stitches around the edges, matching the thread colour to the fabric if needed. Try not to sew through the paper shapes.

8 When all the shapes are sewn in place remove the paper shapes. From the back of the background fabric cut only through the fabric behind each appliqué and coax out the paper shapes. Use tweezers if needed. Press the work. If the cut-up edges on the back don't sit smoothly, fix them to the middle of the appliqué with a little glue.

9 Make a quilt sandwich of the patchwork, wadding (batting) and lining fabric (if using). Quilt as desired. Sew the insect legs and antennae with dark grey thread and small quilting stitches. Trim the work down to 22½in x 13½in (57cm x 34.3cm).

10 The pillow is assembled with an overlapped back, with buttons to secure. Use the two pieces of back fabric and follow the instructions in General Techniques: Button-Fastening Cushion. To finish, use the prepared binding to bind the cushion edge (see General Techniques: Binding).

BEEHIVE PINCUSHIONS

These cute beehive shapes are perfect for pincushions, or just fun decorations. Three colour variations of the large beehive are shown and two of the small beehive. The different sizes are made using the same method.

Finished Sizes
Large: 5½in x 7in (14cm x 18cm)
Small: 3in x 5in (7.6cm x 12.7cm)

MATERIALS
- Print fabrics for circles: fourteen different pieces for large beehive; ten different pieces for small beehive (see Step 2)
- Toy stuffing
- Glue or hot glue gun (optional)
- Flower stick (if mounting on a stick)

Making a Beehive

1 Before you start, refer to the notes in General Techniques: Making Softies. Copy the pattern pieces from the Patterns section and cut out the shapes. Note: The large beehive has seven circles and the small beehive has five circles. It is best to cut squares of fabric (two for each circle size) and then mark and sew the circles on these squares.

2 The various beehives shown use fabrics from the Bumblebee collection. See the Bumblebee Quilt, **Fig A** for the fabric swatches.
For the large beehive, you will need fourteen different pieces, ranging in size from about 7in (17.8cm) square to 3¼in (8.2cm) square.
For the small beehive, you will need ten different pieces, ranging in size from about 4in (10.2cm) square to 2½in (6.4cm) square.

3 To make a beehive, start with the largest circle, placing two different fabric squares right sides together. Draw the large circle pattern and sew on the line (**Fig A**). Cut out with a seam allowance. Cut a slit through one of the fabric layers. Turn through and press (**Fig B**). Repeat this with all circles. To avoid the beehive looking like just a stack of cushions, it's important that there is only filling around the edges, so the circle has the shape of a wheel. Start filling a circle, pushing the filling against the edge of the circle. When the edge is filled in one area, hold the filling in place with tacking (basting) stitches (**Fig C**). Continue filling around the circle. Leave the tacking in place. Repeat on all circles except the top one, which can be fully stuffed.

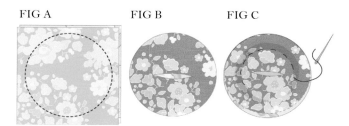

FIG A   FIG B   FIG C

4 Place the circles one on top of the other as in **Fig D**. Make sure the slits you made for turning are hidden by placing the top part with the opening *down*, and the bottom part with the opening *up*. Fabric can stretch a little when it's filled, so when the parts are placed on top of each other, adjust if necessary before fastening together. Fasten the circles together with glue or tacking (basting).

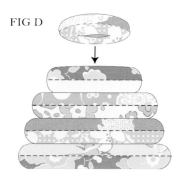

FIG D

BEEHIVE ON A STICK

For a beehive on a stick, push the pointy end of a flower stick against the bottom of the beehive. Turn and press until you pierce the fabric. Continue through a few fabric layers until the beehive sits on the stick securely. Use air-drying clay, oasis or similar to mount the stick in a cup, or push it into a flowerpot.

BUSY BEES

Making these delightful little bees is pleasurably addictive and they look so cute with the beehive pincushions. They only use scraps of fabrics and are really easy to make.

Finished Size 4in x 3½in (10.2cm x 9cm)

MATERIALS
- Print fabric for one body 7in x 5in (17.8cm x 12.7cm)
- Print fabric for two wings 7in x 5in (17.8cm x 12.7cm)
- Wadding (batting) 3½in x 5in (9cm x 12.7cm)
- Toy stuffing

Making a Bee

1 Before you start, refer to the notes in General Techniques: Making Softies. Copy the relevant pattern pieces from the Patterns section and cut out the shapes.

2 A single bee only uses two print fabrics – one for the body and one for the wings. To make the body, fold the body fabric in half, right sides together, and press. Place the body pattern on the fabric and draw around the shape. Mark the gap with dots. Sew on the marked line, leaving a gap (**Fig A**). Cut out the shape with ¼in (6mm) all round for a seam allowance.

3 To make the wings, fold the wing fabric in half, right sides together, and press. Place the wadding (batting) under the fabric layers. Place the wing pattern on the fabric and draw around the shape. Draw a second wing with the pattern reversed (flipped). Sew on the marked lines (**Fig B**).

4 Cut out the shapes with a ¼in (6mm) seam allowance all round. Cut a slit through one of the fabric layers of each wing (**Fig C**). Turn the body through to the right side and press. Stuff and sew up the gap. Turn the wings through to the right side, press and sew up the slits (**Fig D**). To finish, sew the wings to the top of the body (**Fig E**).

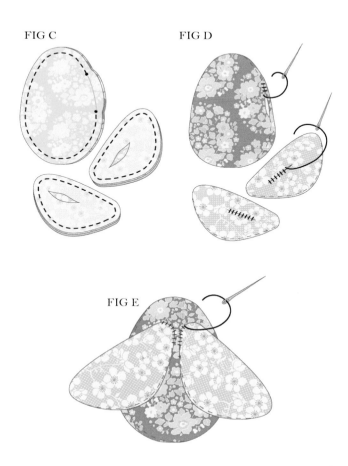

FIG C   FIG D

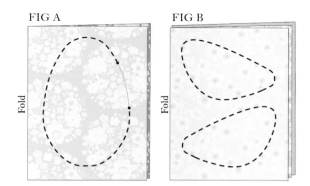

FIG A   FIG B

Fold

Fold

FIG E

FLOWER QUILT

Welcome the summertime with this oh-so-pretty quilt scattered with patchwork flowers. It uses a lovely mix of floral-themed fabrics from the Harvest, Cottage, Bumblebee and Circus collections.

Finished Size 54in x 78in (137cm x 198cm)

FIG A
Fabric swatches
If you can't get hold of one or more of these fabrics,
just replace with fabrics in similar colours

Fabric 1
Solid
off-white

Fabric 2
Flower Tree
ginger

Fabric 3
Bessie
purple

Fabric 4
Bessie
blue

Fabric 5
Flower Bush
teal

Fabric 6
Flower Bush
green

Fabric 7
Flower Tree
green

Fabric 8
Flower Bush
pink

Fabric 9
Bessie
ginger

Fabric 10
Cabbage Flower
green

Fabric 11
Berry Leaf red

Fabric 12
Sigrid
plum

Fabric 13
Berry Leaf
sage

Fabric 14
Botanical
sage

Fabric 15
Flower Nest
ginger

Fabric 16
Cherry Blossom
teal

Fabric 17
Flower Nest
teal

Fabric 18
Garden Bees
green

Fabric 19
Flower Nest
pink

Fabric 20
Forget Me Not
teal

Fabric 21
Summer Picnic
teal

MATERIALS

- Fabric 1: 2½yd (2.3m) – Solid off-white
- Fabric 2: ⅜yd (40cm) – Flower Tree ginger
- Fabric 3: ¼yd (25cm) – Bessie purple
- Fabric 4: ¼yd (25cm) – Bessie blue
- Fabric 5: ¼yd (25cm) – Flower Bush teal
- Fabric 6: ¼yd (25cm) – Flower Bush green
- Fabric 7: ¼yd (25cm) – Flower Tree green
- Fabric 8: ¼yd (25cm) – Flower Bush pink
- Fabric 9: ¼yd (25cm) – Bessie ginger
- Fabric 10: ¼yd (25cm) – Cabbage Flower green
- Fabric 11: ⅜yd (40cm) – Berry Leaf red
- Fabric 12: ¼yd (25cm) – Sigrid plum
- Fabric 13: ¼yd (25cm) – Berry Leaf sage
- Fabric 14: ¼yd (25cm) – Botanical sage
- Fabric 15: ⅜yd (40cm) – Flower Nest ginger
- Fabric 16: ⅛yd (15cm) – Cherry Blossom teal
- Fabric 17: ⅛yd (15cm) – Flower Nest teal
- Fabric 18: ¼yd (25cm) – Garden Bees green
- Fabric 19: ⅜yd (40cm) – Flower Nest pink
- Fabric 20: ¼yd (25cm) – Forget Me Not teal
- Fabric 21: ¼yd (25cm) – Summer Picnic teal
- Backing fabric 3½yds (3.25m) of standard width
- Wadding (batting) 62in x 86in (157.5cm x 218.5cm)
- Binding fabric ½yd (50cm) – Flower Bush teal
- 6½in square quilter's ruler (optional)

Preparation and Cutting Out

1 Before you start, refer to the notes in General Techniques: Making Quilts and Pillows. In this quilt there are 117 blocks – fifty-nine Flower blocks (in eight different colourways), alternating with fifty-eight Leaf blocks (in eight different colourways). The fabrics used for the quilt are shown in **Fig A** and the quilt layout in **Fig B**.

2 From Fabric 1 cut ten 3½in (8.9cm) x width of fabric strips. Sub-cut these into 118 squares 3½in (8.9cm). Cut each square in half once along the diagonal for a total of 236 triangles, for the Flower blocks.

3 From Fabric 1 cut five 3⅜in (8.6cm) x width of fabric strips. Sub-cut these into fifty-eight 3⅜in (8.6cm) squares, for half-square triangle units in the Leaf blocks.

FIG B
Quilt layout

Flower 1	Leaf 6	Flower 2	Leaf 7	Flower 3	Leaf 8	Flower 4	Leaf 5	Flower 1	Row 1
Leaf 1	Flower 5	Leaf 2	Flower 6	Leaf 3	Flower 7	Leaf 4	Flower 8	Leaf 1	Row 2
Flower 4	Leaf 5	Flower 1	Leaf 6	Flower 2	Leaf 7	Flower 3	Leaf 8	Flower 4	Row 3
Leaf 4	Flower 8	Leaf 1	Flower 5	Leaf 2	Flower 6	Leaf 3	Flower 7	Leaf 4	Row 4
Flower 3	Leaf 8	Flower 4	Leaf 5	Flower 1	Leaf 6	Flower 2	Leaf 7	Flower 3	Row 5
Leaf 3	Flower 7	Leaf 4	Flower 8	Leaf 1	Flower 5	Leaf 2	Flower 6	Leaf 3	Row 6
Flower 2	Leaf 7	Flower 3	Leaf 8	Flower 4	Leaf 5	Flower 1	Leaf 6	Flower 2	Row 7
Leaf 2	Flower 6	Leaf 3	Flower 7	Leaf 4	Flower 8	Leaf 1	Flower 5	Leaf 2	Row 8
Flower 1	Leaf 6	Flower 2	Leaf 7	Flower 3	Leaf 8	Flower 4	Leaf 5	Flower 1	Row 9
Leaf 1	Flower 5	Leaf 2	Flower 6	Leaf 3	Flower 7	Leaf 4	Flower 8	Leaf 1	Row 10
Flower 4	Leaf 5	Flower 1	Leaf 6	Flower 2	Leaf 7	Flower 3	Leaf 8	Flower 4	Row 11
Leaf 4	Flower 8	Leaf 1	Flower 5	Leaf 2	Flower 6	Leaf 3	Flower 7	Leaf 4	Row 12
Flower 3	Leaf 8	Flower 4	Leaf 5	Flower 1	Leaf 6	Flower 2	Leaf 7	Flower 3	Row 13

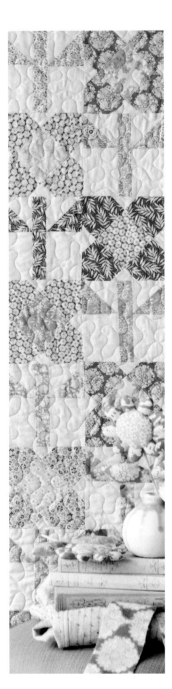

4 From Fabric 1 cut nine 4in (10.2cm) x width of fabric strips. Sub-cut these into 116 pieces 3in x 4in (7.6cm x 10.2cm), for the Leaf blocks.

5 From the following fabrics cut 3½in (8.9cm) squares.
• Fabric 2 cut thirty-six.
• Fabric 3 cut twenty-four.
• Fabric 8 cut twenty-four.
• Fabric 9 cut twenty-four.
• Fabric 11 cut thirty-six.
• Fabric 12 cut twenty-four.
• Fabric 14 cut seventeen.
• Fabric 15 cut thirty-two.
• Fabric 16 cut six.
• Fabric 17 cut six.
• Fabric 19 cut thirty-six.
• Fabric 21 cut fifteen.

6 From Fabric 4 cut the following.
• Nine 3½in (8.9cm) squares.
• Seven 3⅜in (8.6cm) squares.
• Seven 1½in x 6½in (3.8cm x 16.5cm) pieces.

7 From Fabric 5 cut the following.
• Six 3½in (8.9cm) squares.
• Seven 3⅜in (8.6cm) squares.
• Seven 1½in x 6½in (3.8cm x 16.5cm) pieces.

8 From Fabric 6 cut the following.
• Eight 3⅜in (8.6cm) squares.
• Eight 1½in x 6½in (3.8cm x 16.5cm) pieces.

9 From Fabric 7 cut the following.
• Eight 3⅜in (8.6cm) squares.
• Eight 1½in x 6½in (3.8cm x 16.5cm) pieces.

10 From Fabric 10 cut the following.
• Seven 3⅜in (8.6cm) squares.
• Seven 1½in x 6½in (3.8cm x 16.5cm) pieces.

11 From Fabric 13 cut the following.
• Seven 3⅜in (8.6cm) squares.
• Seven 1½in x 6½in (3.8cm x 16.5cm) pieces.

12 From Fabric 18 cut the following.
• Seven 3⅜in (8.6cm) squares.
• Seven 1½in x 6½in (3.8cm x 16.5cm) pieces.

13 From Fabric 20 cut the following.
• Seven 3⅜in (8.6cm) squares.
• Seven 1½in x 6½in (3.8cm x 16.5cm) pieces.

14 Cut the backing fabric across the width into two equal pieces. Sew together along the long side and press open. Trim to a piece about 62in x 86in (157.5cm x 218.5cm).

15 For the binding, from Fabric 5 cut seven 2½in (6.4cm) x width of fabric strips.

Making the Flower Blocks

16 All fifty-nine Flower blocks are made the same way but in eight different fabric combinations. Flower block 1 is described in detail here. Start by taking four 3½in (8.9cm) squares of Fabric 11, one 3½in (8.9cm) square of Fabric 4 and four 3½in (8.9cm) triangles of off-white. Place them in the layout shown in **Fig C** and sew them together in rows. Don't worry if the point of the triangle doesn't meet the edge of the square, as this part will be cut off soon. Press seams open or to one side. Now sew the three rows together and press. Rotate the pieced unit 45 degrees, as in **Fig D** and place a 6½in square quilting ruler over the unit so it is exactly in the centre (vertically and horizontally). Carefully cut out the 6½in (16.5cm) square (see Tip).

FIG C

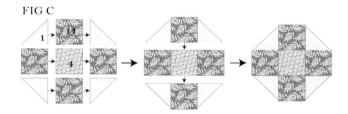

FIG D

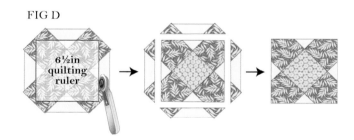

TIP If you don't have a square quilting ruler, measure the square with your normal quilting ruler. Alternatively, you could create a 6½in (16.5cm) square template from template plastic and use this to mark the square.

17 Follow this same process to make the rest of the Flower blocks, following the fabric combinations and numbers of blocks given in **Fig E**.

FIG E

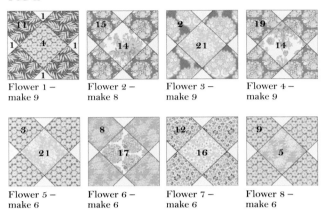

Flower 1 – make 9 Flower 2 – make 8 Flower 3 – make 9 Flower 4 – make 9

Flower 5 – make 6 Flower 6 – make 6 Flower 7 – make 6 Flower 8 – make 6

Making the Leaf Blocks

18 All fifty-eight Leaf blocks are made the same way but in eight different fabric combinations. Leaf block 1 is described in detail here.

19 Make the half-square triangle (HST) units as follows. Place one 3⅜in (8.6cm) square of off-white right sides together with one square of Fabric 6 (**Fig F**). Mark a diagonal line across the off-white square. Sew a line ¼in (6mm) away from both sides of the line. Cut the fabrics apart along the marked line and press the units open. Check the units are 3in (7.6cm) square.

FIG F

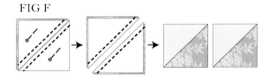

20 Take the two HSTs just made plus two 3in x 4in (7.6cm x 10.2cm) pieces of off-white and one 1½in x 6½in (3.8cm x 16.5cm) piece of Fabric 6. Sew the pieces together as shown in **Fig G** and press. Check the block is 6½in (16.5cm) square.

FIG G

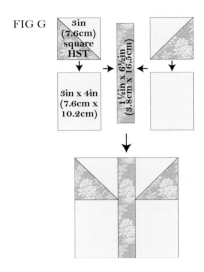

21 Follow the steps above to make the rest of the Leaf blocks, following the fabric combinations and numbers of blocks given in **Fig H**.

FIG H

Leaf 1 – make 8 Leaf 2 – make 7 Leaf 3 – make 7 Leaf 4 – make 8

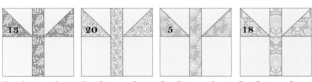

Leaf 5 – make 7 Leaf 6 – make 7 Leaf 7 – make 7 Leaf 8 – make 7

Assembling the Quilt

22 Lay out the Flower blocks and Leaf blocks in the order shown in quilt layout **Fig B**. Sew the blocks together row by row. Press the seams in alternate rows in opposite directions. Now sew the rows together, matching seams neatly. Press long seams open or to one side.

Quilting and Finishing

23 Make a quilt sandwich of the backing fabric, wadding (batting) and quilt. Quilt as desired. Square up the quilt, trimming excess wadding and backing.

24 Use the prepared binding to bind your quilt – see General Techniques: Binding. Add a label to your beautiful quilt to finish.

FLOWER PILLOWS

*These two pillows are inspired by the Flower Quilt and use some of the same fabrics, so refer to the fabric swatches in **Fig A** of the quilt. Instructions and materials are given for the long pillow. The short pillow uses the same techniques but different fabrics and fewer blocks. Note that some of the Leaf blocks have been rearranged for these cushions.*

Finished Sizes
Long pillow: 36in x 18in (91.4cm x 45.7cm)
Short pillow: 24in x 18in (61cm x 45.7cm)

MATERIALS

Long Flower Pillow
- Fabric 1: ½yd (50cm) – Solid off-white
- Small pieces of the print fabrics – maximum of 7in (17.8cm) square each
- Wadding (batting) 38in x 20in (96.5cm x 50.8cm)
- Lining fabric 38in x 20in (96.5cm x 50.8cm) (optional)
- Fabric for back of cushion, two pieces 22in x 18½in (56cm x 47cm)
- Three buttons for pillow back (optional)

LONG FLOWER PILLOW

1 From Fabric 1 cut the following pieces.
- Twelve 3½in (8.9cm) squares.
- Twenty-four pieces 3in x 4in (7.6cm x 10.2cm).
- Twelve 3⅜in (8.6cm) squares.

2 Cut 3½in (8.9cm) squares from the following fabrics.
- One from Fabrics 4, 5, 16 and 21.
- Two from Fabric 14.
- Four from Fabrics 2, 9, 11, 12, 15 and 19.

3 Cut two 1½in x 6½in (3.8cm x 16.5cm) pieces from Fabrics 4, 5, 6, 7, 10 and 18.

4 Cut two 3⅜in (8.6cm) squares from Fabrics 4, 5, 6, 7, 10 and 18.

5 To make the long pillow, follow the Flower Quilt instructions to make the Flower blocks, making one each of block 1, 2, 3, 4, 7 and 8. **Fig A** here shows the blocks and the fabrics used.

FIG A

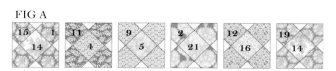

Flower 2   Flower 1   Flower 8   Flower 3   Flower 7   Flower 4

6 Follow the Flower Quilt instructions to make the Leaf blocks, making two each of block 1, 2, 3, 4, 7 and 8. Note: For this cushion, Leaf blocks 3, 4 and 8 need to have their units rearranged *before* the block is assembled, so the layout of the blocks appear as in **Fig B** here.

FIG B

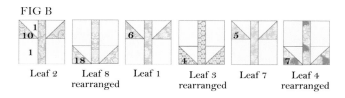

Leaf 2   Leaf 8 rearranged   Leaf 1   Leaf 3 rearranged   Leaf 7   Leaf 4 rearranged

7 Place the blocks in rows in the order in **Fig C** here. Sew together and press. Sew the rows together and press.

FIG C

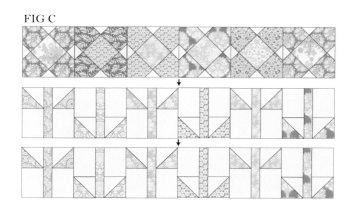

8 Make a quilt sandwich of the patchwork, wadding (batting) and lining fabric (if using). Quilt as desired.

9 The pillow is assembled with an overlapped back, with buttons to secure. Use the two pieces of fabric for the cushion back and follow the instructions in General Techniques: Button-Fastening Cushion. This pillow doesn't have a bound edge.

SHORT FLOWER PILLOW

This pillow uses just four Flower blocks and eight Leaf blocks from the Flower Quilt. Follow **Fig D** and **Fig E** here for the blocks and **Fig F** here for the pillow assembly. Note: Leaf blocks 4 and 6 need to have their units rearranged *before* the block is assembled. Once pieced, the patchwork is 24½in x 18½in (62.2cm x 47cm). Make a quilt sandwich and quilt as desired. Make up the cushion in the same way as the Long Pillow, using fabric pieces suitable for the size of this pillow. This pillow doesn't have a bound edge.

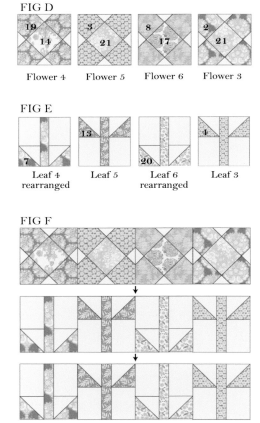

FIG D

Flower 4   Flower 5   Flower 6   Flower 3

FIG E

Leaf 4 rearranged   Leaf 5   Leaf 6 rearranged   Leaf 3

FIG F

FABRIC FLOWERS

*These pretty flowers are easy to sew and make really charming decorations. They only use small amounts of fabrics – the flowers shown use fabrics from the Bumblebee collection (see **Fig A** of the Bumblebee Quilt for the swatches).*

Finished Size 4in x 4in (10.2cm x 10.2cm) (flowerhead only)

MATERIALS
- Print fabric for petals 15in x 10in (38cm x 25.5cm)
- Print fabric for flower centre 7in x 3½in (17.8cm x 9cm)
- Print fabric for leaves 6½in x 6½in (16.5cm x 16.5cm)
- Toy stuffing
- Flower stick
- Air-drying clay, oasis or similar
- Flowerpot or teacup

Making a Flower

1 Before you start, refer to the notes in General Techniques: Making Softies. Copy the relevant pattern pieces from the Patterns section and cut out the shapes.

2 To make the petals, fold the petal fabric in half, right sides together. Draw the three-petal pattern on the fabric three times. Sew on the lines (no gap is needed). Cut out each shape with a seam allowance. Carefully cut a slit through one of the fabric layers (**Fig A**). Turn through, press and stuff. For the petals to lie properly do not put stuffing into the centre.

3 To make the centre, fold the fabric in half, right sides together and draw the circle. Sew on the line. Cut out with a seam allowance. Cut a slit through one fabric layer (**Fig B**). Turn through and press. Stuff lightly, sew up the slit and press a little to make the centre a nice shape.

4 To make a leaf, fold the leaf fabric in half, right sides together. Draw the leaf pattern and sew on the line, leaving a gap for turning (**Fig C**). Cut out with a seam allowance, turn through, press, stuff and sew up the gap.

FIG C

5 To assemble the flower, put the petal pieces on top of each other with the reverse openings facing each other. Rotate the pieces to achieve a balanced look. Put the flower centre on top, slit facing down. Fix together with pins and then sew together all round the centre (**Fig D**).

6 To mount on a stick, push and turn the pointy end of the flower stick through the narrowest part of the leaf piece first – to make sure you don't pierce the seam, keep a little to the back of the piece. Coax the stick through the turning opening on the rearmost petal piece and up through one of the petals (**Fig E**). Use air-drying clay, oasis or similar to mount the stick in a teacup, or push it into a flowerpot.

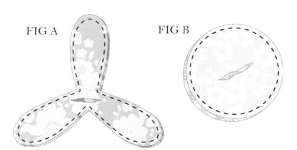

FIG A   FIG B

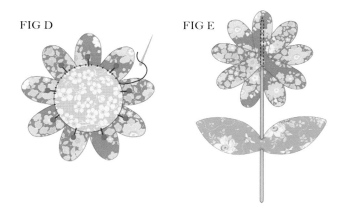

FIG D   FIG E

CIRCUS QUILT

This fun and colourful quilt has five different blocks that create a really attractive arrangement. It's a challenge but the finished result is so worth the effort and will be loved for many years to come. It uses fabrics from the cheerful Circus collection.

Finished Size 54in x 76½in (137cm x 194cm)

FIG A
Fabric swatches
If you can't get hold of one or more of these fabrics, just replace with fabrics in similar colours

 Fabric 1
Solid
off-white

 Fabric 9
Circus Rose
blue

 Fabric 2
Clown Flower
teal

 Fabric 10
Summer Picnic
blue

 Fabric 3
Forget Me Not
teal

 Fabric 11
Clown Flower
blue)

 Fabric 4
First Kiss
teal

 Fabric 12
First Kiss
blue

 Fabric 5
Summer Picnic
teal

 Fabric 13
First Kiss
green

 Fabric 6
Circus Rose
teal

 Fabric 14
Circus Rose
green

 Fabric 7
Forget Me Not
blue

 Fabric 15
Forget Me Not
green

 Fabric 8
Circus Rose
red

MATERIALS
- Fabric 1: 3yd (2.75m) – Solid off-white
- Fabric 2: ¼yd (25cm) – Clown Flower teal
- Fabric 3: ½yd (50cm) – Forget Me Not teal
- Fabric 4: ¼yd (25cm) – First Kiss teal
- Fabric 5: ¾yd (70cm) – Summer Picnic teal
- Fabric 6: ⅜yd (40cm) – Circus Rose teal
- Fabric 7: ¼yd (25cm) – Forget Me Not blue
- Fabric 8: ½yd (50cm) – Circus Rose red
- Fabric 9: ¼yd (25cm) – Circus Rose blue
- Fabric 10: ⅛yd (15cm) – Summer Picnic blue
- Fabric 11: ¼yd (25cm) – Clown Flower blue
- Fabric 12: ¼yd (25cm) – First Kiss blue
- Fabric 13: ¼yd (25cm) – First Kiss green
- Fabric 14: ⅜yd (40cm) – Circus Rose green
- Fabric 15: ¼yd (25cm) – Forget Me Not green
- Backing fabric 3½yd (3.25m) of standard width
- Wadding (batting) 63in x 85in (160cm x 215cm)
- Binding fabric ½yd (50cm) – Forget Me Not blue
- Sixteen ¾in (2cm) diameter fabric-covered buttons (for example, Forget Me Not Green)

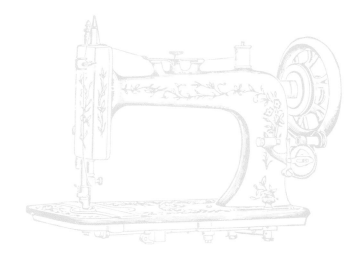

1 Before you start, refer to the notes in General Techniques: Making Quilts and Pillows. There are 204 blocks in the quilt in total, in a 12 x 17 block layout. There are five different blocks, each 5in (12.7cm) square (unfinished). The fabrics used for the quilt are shown in **Fig A** and the quilt layout in **Fig B**. The blocks are identified in **Fig C**.

FIG C

Flying Geese

Friendship Star

Nine-Patch

Striped

Circus Wagon

FIG B
The eight different Flying Geese blocks are identified, showing where they are rotated

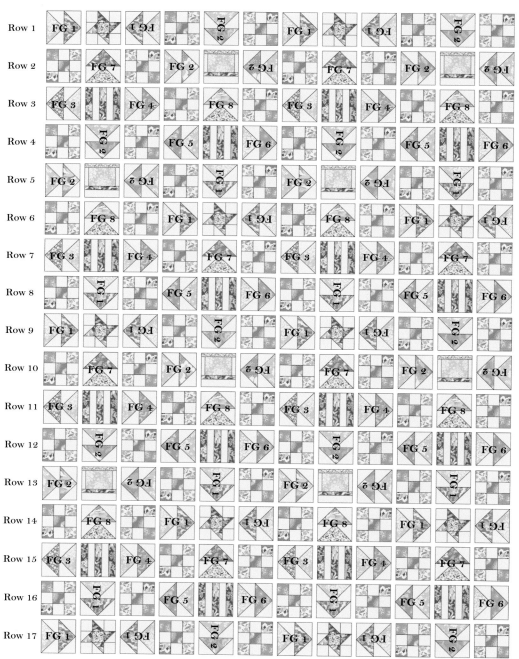

38

2 The specific cutting instructions are given for the five different blocks, as it is easier to cut fabrics and make the different blocks as you go along.

3 From the binding fabric cut seven 2½in (6.4cm) x width of fabric strips. Sew the strips together end to end and press seams open. Press the binding in half along the length, wrong sides together.

Making the Flying Geese Blocks

4 There are 102 Flying Geese blocks in the quilt, with each block made up of two flying geese units. One unit is 2¾in x 5in (7cm x 12.7cm) (unfinished) and two units sewn together make a 5in (12.7cm) square block (unfinished). **Fig B** gives the specific positions of all of the Flying Geese blocks. Note that some of the blocks are rotated. There are eight different colour combinations of Flying Geese (FG) blocks – see **Fig D** for the specific fabrics used and number of blocks to make.

FIG D

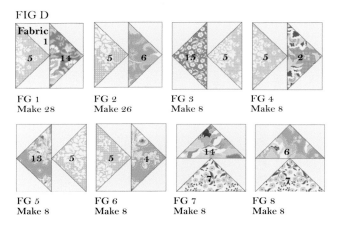

FG 1
Make 28

FG 2
Make 26

FG 3
Make 8

FG 4
Make 8

FG 5
Make 8

FG 6
Make 8

FG 7
Make 8

FG 8
Make 8

5 For speed, the flying geese units are made using a four-at-once method. The background squares need to be cut 5¾in (14.6cm) and the corner squares cut 3⅛in (7.9cm).

6 For the FG1 blocks cut the following.
• Fabric 1 cut twenty-eight 3⅛in (7.9cm) squares.
• Fabric 5 cut seven 5¾in (14.6cm) squares.
• Fabric 1 cut twenty-eight 3⅛in (7.9cm) squares.
• Fabric 14 cut seven 5¾in (14.6cm) squares.

7 For the FG2 blocks cut the following (there will be some spare units).
• Fabric 1 cut twenty-eight 3⅛in (7.9cm) squares.
• Fabric 5 cut seven 5¾in (14.6cm) squares.
• Fabric 1 cut twenty-eight 3⅛in (7.9cm) squares.
• Fabric 6 cut seven 5¾in (14.6cm) squares.

8 For the FG3 blocks cut the following.
• Fabric 1 cut eight 3⅛in (7.9cm) squares.
• Fabric 15 cut two 5¾in (14.6cm) squares.
• Fabric 1 cut eight 3⅛in (7.9cm) squares.
• Fabric 5 cut two 5¾in (14.6cm) squares.

9 For the FG4 blocks cut the following.
• Fabric 1 cut eight 3⅛in (7.9cm) squares.
• Fabric 5 cut two 5¾in (14.6cm) squares.
• Fabric 1 cut eight 3⅛in (7.9cm) squares.
• Fabric 2 cut two 5¾in (14.6cm) squares.

10 For the FG5 blocks cut the following.
• Fabric 1 cut eight 3⅛in (7.9cm) squares.
• Fabric 13 cut two 5¾in (14.6cm) squares.
• Fabric 1 cut eight 3⅛in (7.9cm) squares.
• Fabric 5 cut two 5¾in (14.6cm) squares.

11 For the FG6 blocks cut the following.
• Fabric 1 cut eight 3⅛in (7.9cm) squares.
• Fabric 5 cut two 5¾in (14.6cm) squares.
• Fabric 1 cut eight 3⅛in (7.9cm) squares.
• Fabric 4 cut two 5¾in (14.6cm) squares.

12 For the FG7 blocks cut the following.
• Fabric 1 cut eight 3⅛in (7.9cm) squares.
• Fabric 14 cut two 5¾in (14.6cm) squares.
• Fabric 1 cut eight 3⅛in (7.9cm) squares.
• Fabric 7 cut two 5¾in (14.6cm) squares.

13 For the FG8 blocks cut the following.
• Fabric 1 cut eight 3⅛in (7.9cm) squares.
• Fabric 6 cut two 5¾in (14.6cm) squares.
• Fabric 1 cut eight 3⅛in (7.9cm) squares.
• Fabric 7 cut two 5¾in (14.6cm) squares.

14 Make the flying geese units as described in General Techniques: Flying Geese – Four at Once. To make FG1, select a Fabric 5 large square and four Fabric 1 small squares. Once made, check each unit is 2¾in x 5in (7cm x 12.7cm). Repeat this process with a Fabric 14 large square and four Fabric 1 small squares to make another four units.

15 To assemble a block, take a Fabric 1+5 unit and sew it together with a Fabric 1+14 unit, along the long seam. Press the seam and check the block is 5in (12.7cm) square. Repeat with the remaining units to make twenty-eight FG1s altogether. Label and put the blocks aside.

16 Repeat this process to make the remaining Flying Geese blocks. Keep the same blocks together and label them, so you can find them easily later.

Making the Friendship Star Blocks

17 The ten Friendship Star blocks in the quilt are all made the same way, using the same three fabrics: Fabric 1, Fabric 7 and Fabric 8 – see **Fig E**.

For the Friendship Star blocks cut the following.
• Fabric 1 cut forty 2in (5cm) squares.
• Fabric 7 cut ten 2in (5cm) squares.
• Fabric 8 cut ten 3½in (8.9cm) squares for HST units.
• Fabric 1 cut ten 3½in (8.9cm) squares for HST units.

FIG E

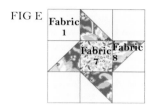

18 The ten Friendship Star blocks need forty HST units in total (four per block) and these are best made using a four-at-once method – see General Techniques: Half-Square Triangles – Four at Once. Use a Fabric 1 and a Fabric 8 3½in (8.9cm) square. Once made, check each unit is 2in (5cm) square, trimming as needed. Repeat this process with the other squares of Fabric 1 and Fabric 8, to make forty HSTs in total.

19 Following **Fig F**, sew a Friendship Star block together. Press seams open. Check the block is 5in (12.7cm) square. Repeat to create ten blocks in total.

FIG F

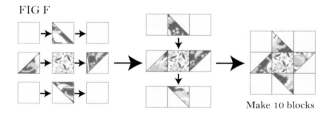

Make 10 blocks

Making the Nine-Patch Blocks

20 The sixty-eight Nine-Patch blocks are all made in the same way but half of them are rotated 180 degrees before being sewn into the quilt. The blocks are quickly made with strip piecing. Five fabrics are used for these blocks (shown in **Fig G**) – Fabrics 1, 3, 9, 11 and 12.

FIG G

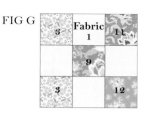

21 For the Nine-Patch blocks cut the following pieces.
• Fabric 1 cut sixteen 2in (5cm) x width of fabric strips.
• Fabric 3 cut eight 2in (5cm) x width of fabric strips.
• Fabric 9 cut four 2in (5cm) x width of fabric strips.
• Fabric 11 cut four 2in (5cm) x width of fabric strips.
• Fabric 12 cut four 2in (5cm) x width of fabric strips.

22 The blocks are made from three different strip-pieced units. **Fig H** shows which fabrics make up these units. For each of the units, sew the strips together along the long sides and press seams open. The depth of each sewn unit should be 5in (12.7cm). Repeat to make four of each unit.

FIG H

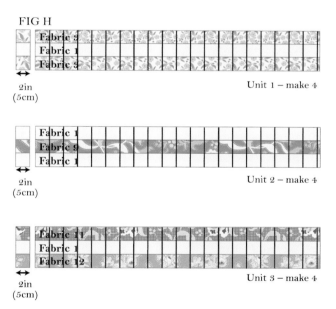

2in (5cm) — Unit 1 – make 4

2in (5cm) — Unit 2 – make 4

2in (5cm) — Unit 3 – make 4

23 Taking each strip-pieced unit in turn, cut the long unit into segments 2in (5cm) wide (twenty-one from each unit). This will give you a total of eighty-four Unit 1 segments, eighty-four Unit 2 segments and eighty-four Unit 3 segments. (Note: Some segments will be spare, which you could use for cushions if you like.)

24 To assemble a block, sew the units together as in **Fig I**, aligning seams. Press seams open. Check the block is 5in (12.7cm) square. Repeat to create sixty-eight blocks in total.

FIG I

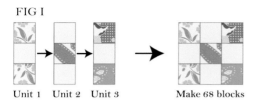

Unit 1   Unit 2   Unit 3   Make 68 blocks

Making the Striped Blocks

25 There are sixteen Striped blocks in the quilt and they are most efficiently made with strip piecing. Just two fabrics are used for all of these blocks – Fabric 1 and Fabric 8. For the Striped blocks cut the following pieces.
- Fabric 1 cut four 1⅜in (3.5cm) x width of fabric strips.
- Fabric 8 cut six 1⅜in (3.5cm) x width of fabric strips.

26 Following **Fig J**, take two strips of Fabric 1 and three strips of Fabric 8 and sew them together along the long edges in an alternating order, using a *scant* ¼in (6mm) seam allowance. Press the seams open. Check that the strip-pieced unit is 5in (12.7cm) deep – if it isn't, then reduce your seam allowance a little more. Make a second strip-pieced unit in the same way. Cut the first strip-pieced unit into 5in wide segments. Repeat with the second unit. You should get eight blocks from each unit, so sixteen blocks in total. Put the blocks aside for the moment.

FIG J

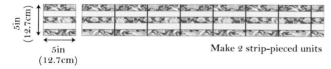

5in (12.7cm)

5in (12.7cm)   Make 2 strip-pieced units

Making the Circus Wagon Blocks

27 There are eight Circus Wagon blocks in the quilt, each made up of variable pieces to create the wagon-shaped block (see **Fig K**). Each block uses the same fabrics – Fabric 7, 10, 8 and 1, plus ¾in (2cm) diameter buttons.
For the Circus Wagon blocks cut the following pieces.
- Fabric 7 cut eight 5in x 1in (12.7cm x 2.5cm).
- Fabric 10 cut eight 4in x 3in (10.2cm x 7.6cm).
- Fabric 8 cut eight 5in x 1in (12.7cm x 2.5cm).
- Fabric 1 cut eight 5in x 1½in (12.7cm x 3.8cm).
- Fabric 1 cut sixteen 1in x 3in (2.5cm x 7.6cm).

FIG K

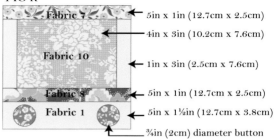

Fabric 7 ← 5in x 1in (12.7cm x 2.5cm)
← 4in x 3in (10.2cm x 7.6cm)
Fabric 10 ← 1in x 3in (2.5cm x 7.6cm)
Fabric 8 ← 5in x 1in (12.7cm x 2.5cm)
Fabric 1 ← 5in x 1½in (12.7cm x 3.8cm)
← ¾in (2cm) diameter button

28 Assemble the block following the stages in **Fig L** and pressing seams open. Check the sewn block is 5in (12.7cm) square. Repeat this to create eight blocks in total. Each block needs two buttons for 'wheels' but it is best to wait until the quilt is assembled and quilted before adding these.

FIG L

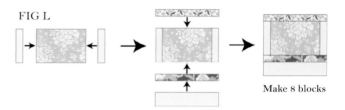

Make 8 blocks

Assembling the Quilt

29 When all of the blocks have been made, lay them out as in **Fig B**. Arrange them correctly, rotating where shown in the diagram. (It will help if you realise that Rows 1 to 8 are repeated in Rows 9 to 16, with an extra Row 1 at the bottom of the quilt.)

30 Sew the blocks together row by row, matching seams carefully. Press the seams in alternate rows in opposite directions. Now sew the rows together, matching seams neatly. Press long seams open or to one side.

Quilting and Finishing

31 Cut the backing fabric across the width into two equal pieces. Sew together along the long side and press the seam open. Trim to a piece about 63in x 85in (160cm x 216cm). Make a quilt sandwich of the backing fabric, wadding (batting) and quilt. Quilt as desired. Sew the buttons on the Circus Wagon blocks. Square up the quilt, trimming excess wadding and backing.

32 Use the prepared binding to bind your quilt – see General Techniques: Binding. Add a label to your gorgeous quilt to finish.

THE DAY THEY WENT TO THE CIRCU

TREE PILLOW

This pillow is created with the slightly more unusual technique of reverse appliqué, where the top fabric is cut away to reveal the bright print below. Our method is a quick one as when the top fabric is cut, there is no need to turn the seam allowance under. A red and blue pillow are shown, with instructions for the red pillow.

Finished Size 25in x 21¼in (63.5cm x 54cm)

MATERIALS

Red Pillow
- Fabric 1: 1½yd (1.5m) – Solid off-white (see Step 2)
- Fabric 2: 26½in x 22¾in (67.3cm x 57.8cm) – Circus Rose red
- Wadding (batting) 26½in x 22¾in (67.3cm x 57.8cm)
- Removable marker pen
- Small, sharp-pointed embroidery scissors

Making the Pillow

1 Before you start, refer to the notes in General Techniques: Making Quilts and Pillows. The pattern is a large one and has been split over several pages in the Patterns section. Join the pattern pieces at the dashed lines to make one vertical half of the design. Draw this half pattern onto one half of a 25in x 22in (63.5cm x 56cm) piece of paper. (For a piece of paper large enough you could tape six sheets of A4 size paper together, or four sheets of A3 size.) Flip the pattern over to draw the other half (see **Fig A**). Make sure the lines of the pattern are thick enough to trace through fabric.

2 Cut Fabric 1 as follows.
- One piece 26½in x 22¾in (67.3cm x 57.8cm) for the top layer. Note: You may need to use two layers of the light fabric, to prevent a dark print showing through. If you do this you will need extra of Fabric 1.
- One piece 26½in x 22¾in (67.3cm x 57.8cm) for backing when quilting. This is optional and can be omitted.
- Two pieces 17in x 21¾in (43.2cm x 55.3cm) for the back of the pillow cover.

3 From Fabric 2 cut one 26½in x 22¾in (67.3cm x 57.8cm).

4 Fold the Fabric 1 top layer piece into quarters to lightly crease the halfway points. This will help you position the appliqué. The background is cut slightly larger to allow for any frayed edges to be trimmed later.

Working the Reverse Appliqué

5 Start by transferring the pattern to the fabric as follows. Place the off-white fabric rectangle right side up with the paper pattern behind it. You should be able to see the pattern through the fabric. Use a removable pen to draw all of the shapes onto the fabric (**Fig B**).

FIG A

FIG B

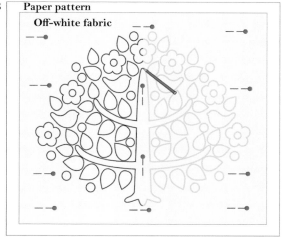

Paper pattern

Off-white fabric

6 Place the second layer of Fabric 1 behind the marked fabric (if you are using two layers). Place the Fabric 2 rectangle right side up behind the off-white rectangle and then the piece of wadding (batting). Pin the layers in place. Using off-white thread (or thread to match the top fabric) machine sew on all of the marked lines, using a slightly shorter stitch length than normal. Take your time with this and sew carefully to follow the shapes accurately, lifting the machine foot to pivot where necessary (**Fig C**). When all sewing is finished, take the thread tails through to the back of the work, tie off and trim. Press the work.

FIG C

7 Use a pair of sharp, pointed embroidery scissors to cut away areas of the top layer of fabric, about ⅛in (2mm–3mm) inside the shapes. You can do this cutting by eye – **Fig D**

shows this in progress. Note that the circles in the centres of the flowers need to be cut *outside* of the sewn circle. If desired, you could wash the cover later to encourage these edges to fray more.

FIG D

Quilting and Finishing

8 Add another piece of Fabric 1 at the back of the work, if desired, and quilt further as you choose. For example, you could echo quilt around the outside of the complete design and also inside the tree and branches. Trim the work down to 25½in x 21¾in (64.8cm x 55.3cm), keeping the design central.

9 The pillow is assembled with an overlapped back, with buttons to secure. Use the two pieces of pillow back fabric and follow the instructions in See General Techniques: Button-Fastening Cushion.

APPLIQUÉ ELEPHANT

These adorable elephants are made with a simple pattern, with paper piece appliqué for the hat and blanket. Additional decoration is created with appliqué perse and patterned buttons. One of the elephants shown is described, but you can use any combination of fabrics.

Finished Size 13½in x 12in (34.3cm x 30.5cm)

MATERIALS

Pale Blue Elephant

- Fabric for elephant: 32in x 16in (81.3cm x 40.6cm) – Summer Picnic teal
- Fabric for rug: 8in x 6½in (20.3cm x 16.5cm) – First Kiss linen
- Fabric for hat: 4in x 4in (10.2cm x 10.2cm) – Circus Rose green
- Fabric for motif appliqué: sufficient to cut out floral motifs – Circus Rose green
- Toy stuffing and wooden stick
- Small, sharp-pointed embroidery scissors
- Paper piece glue
- Buttons – three ½in (15mm) and one 1in (28mm)
- Black hobby paint for eyes

Making the Elephant

1 Before you start, refer to the notes in General Techniques: Making Softies. Copy the pattern pieces from the Patterns section and cut out the shapes. Tape the elephant parts together on the dashed lines.

2 Start by making the appliqués for the hat and blanket. Mark the hat pattern on the hat fabric and cut out with a ¼in (6mm) seam allowance all round (**Fig A**). Snip into tight curves as shown. Place the hat paper pattern on the wrong side of the fabric shape and fold the seam allowance over the edge of the paper. Leave the top of the shape *unturned* – this section needs to stick out so it can be sewn into the seam allowance later. Press or glue the folded edges in place. Repeat this process with the blanket (**Fig B**).

FIG A

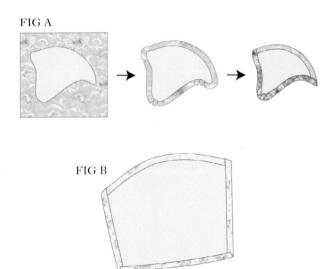

FIG B

3 Take the elephant fabric and fold it in half right sides together so it's 16in (40.6cm) square. Draw the pattern on the back of the fabric and roughly cut out the two elephant shapes – cut a normal amount of seam allowance around the back and head but leave the fabric between the trunk and body and between the legs, as in **Fig C**.

FIG C

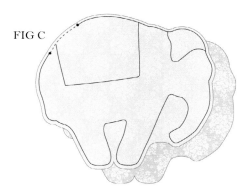

4 Appliqué the hat and the blanket in place on to the right side of the body. To place the appliqués according to the pattern, line up the seam allowance along the top of the elephant (**Fig D**). You could also use pins through the fabric to mark where the lines go. Sew the appliques in place, leaving the top edges free. Now remove the hat and blanket paper patterns – because the top is open you will be able to wiggle out the papers without cutting into the back fabric.

FIG D

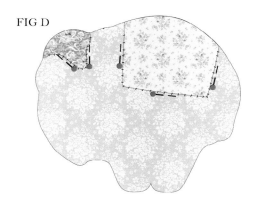

5 Place the two elephant shapes right sides together and sew around on the drawn line, leaving the gap open (**Fig E**). Finely cut out the elephant and cut notches where the seam turns in. Turn through, press and then stuff.

FIG E

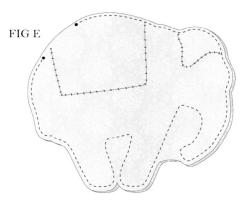

6 Add the flower decorations as follows. Choose two flower motifs from the Circus Rose green fabric. Cut the first motif out with a seam allowance (**Fig F1**). Snip into the seam allowance where it curves. Begin to turn the seam allowance to the wrong side, pressing and then tacking (basting) or gluing into place – you don't have to follow the flower shape exactly. Repeat with the second motif (**Fig F2**). Appliqué the flowers on the edge of the blanket, sewing in place with tiny stitches. Remove tacking (**Fig G**).

FIG F

1

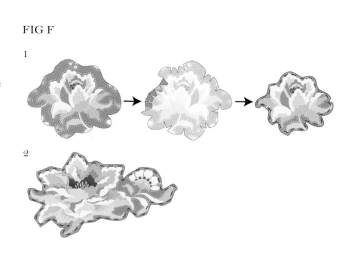

2

FIG G

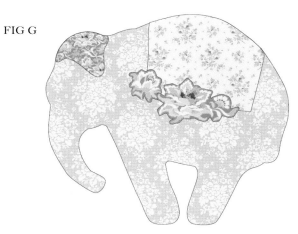

7 Sew on the large button at the bottom of the hat and add the three small buttons on the elephant. To finish, stamp on eyes ¼in (6mm–7mm) in diameter, using a large ball-headed pin and black hobby paint – see General Techniques: Faces.

CABBAGE ROSE QUILT

The patchwork for this quilt is easy to do using strip piecing and is the perfect background for the pretty appliqué. The piecing and appliqué use fabrics from the Cabbage Rose range.

Finished Size 54in x 78in (137cm x 198cm)

FIG A
Fabric swatches
If you can't get hold of one or more of these fabrics, just replace with fabrics in similar colours

Fabric 1
Solid
off-white

Fabric 2
Solid
teal

Fabric 3
Lucille
teal

Fabric 4
Libby
teal

Fabric 5
Flowercloud
teal

Fabric 6
Lucille
red

Fabric 7
Tess
red

Fabric 8
Tilly
red

Fabric 9
Tess
ginger

Fabric 10
Solid
olive

Fabric 11
Solid
ginger

Fabric 12
Solid
pink

MATERIALS
- Fabric 1: 3¼yds (3m) – Solid off-white
- Fabric 2: 1½yds (1.4m) – Solid teal
- Fabric 3: ½yd (50cm) – Lucille teal
- Fabric 4: ¼yd (25cm) – Libby teal
- Fabric 5: ¼yd (25cm) – Flowercloud teal
- Fabric 6: ⅛yd (15cm) – Lucille red
- Fabric 7: ⅛yd (15cm) – Tess red
- Fabric 8: ⅛yd (15cm) – Tilly red
- Fabric 9: ⅛yd (15cm) – Tess ginger
- Fabric 10: ½yd (50cm) – Solid olive
- Fabric 11: ⅛yd (15cm) – Solid ginger
- Fabric 12: ⅜yd (40cm) – Solid pink
- Backing fabric 3½yds (3.25m) of standard width
- Wadding (batting) 62in x 86in (157.5cm x 218.5cm)
- Binding fabric ½yd (50cm) – Tilly red
- Thick coated paper for paper piece appliqué
- Paper piece glue
- Pointy stick and tweezers (optional)

Preparation and Cutting Out

1 The quilt is made up of seven square and six rectangular chequerboard blocks alternating with plain blocks. The plain blocks and the plain border at the top and bottom of the quilt are decorated with appliqué. The appliqué is most easily worked using paper shapes, but you could copy the templates and use them to create your own shapes for needle-turn appliqué if you prefer. See **Fig A** for the fabric swatches and **Fig B** for the quilt layout.

2 From Fabric 1 cut four 15in (38.1cm) x width of fabric strips. Sub-cut these strips as follows.
- Eight 15in (38.1cm) squares for the appliqué blocks. These will be trimmed down later, after the appliqué is worked, to trim off any frayed edges.
- Four 7in x 15in (17.8cm x 38.1cm) rectangles for the appliqué blocks. These will be trimmed down later.
- Keep the spare fabric for the off-white appliqué flowers in the border.

FIG B
Quilt layout

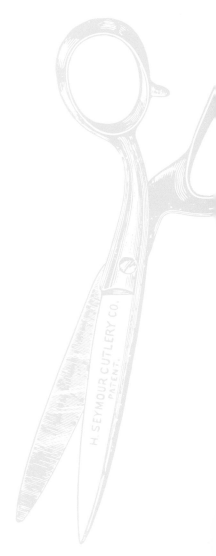

3 From Fabric 1 cut twenty-one 2½in (6.4cm) x width of fabric strips, for the pieced blocks.

4 From Fabric 2 cut twelve 2½in (6.4cm) x width of fabric strips, for the pieced blocks.

5 From Fabric 2 cut four 5in (12.7cm) x width of fabric strips for the appliqué borders. Join two of these strips together end to end and then cut into one length 5in x 55in (12.7cm x 139.7cm), keeping the seam in the centre. Keep the offcuts to use for appliqué. Repeat with the other two strips. These strips will be trimmed slightly later.

6 From each of Fabric 3, Fabric 4 and Fabric 5 cut three 2½in (6.4cm) x width of fabric strips. Keep spare fabric for appliqués.

7 Cut the backing fabric across the width into two equal pieces. Sew together along the long side and press the seam open. Trim to a piece about 62in x 86in (157.5cm x 218.5cm). This is about 4in (10.2cm) larger all round than the quilt top, to allow for quilting and finishing.

8 Cut the binding fabric into seven 2½in (6.4cm) x width of fabric strips. Sew the strips together end to end and press seams open. Press the binding in half along the length, wrong sides together.

Making the Pieced Blocks

9 The checkerboard blocks are most efficiently made with strip piecing and there are four different strip-pieced units needed, made using 2½in (6.4cm) strips as follows. You will have some segments spare.

- To make Strip Unit 1 (**Fig C**) sew together four Fabric 2 strips with three Fabric 1 strips, pressing seams open or to one side. Cut the pieced unit into sixteen 2½in (6.4cm) wide segments, as shown. Make three strip units like this in total.
- To make Strip Unit 2 (**Fig D**) sew together four Fabric 1 strips with one Fabric 3 strip, one Fabric 4 strip and one Fabric 5 strip, in the order shown on the diagram. Cut the pieced unit into sixteen 2½in (6.4cm) wide segments.
- To make Strip Unit 3 (**Fig E**) sew together four Fabric 1 strips with one Fabric 5 strip, one Fabric 3 strip and one Fabric 4 strip, in the order shown. Cut the pieced unit into sixteen 2½in (6.4cm) wide segments.
- To make Strip Unit 4 (**Fig F**) sew together four Fabric 1 strips with one Fabric 4 strip, one Fabric 5 strip and one Fabric 3 strip, in the order shown. Cut the pieced unit into sixteen 2½in (6.4cm) wide segments.

FIG C
Strip Unit 1 – make 3

Fab 2
Fab 1

FIG D
Strip Unit 2 – make 1

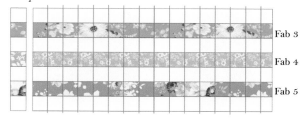

Fab 3
Fab 4
Fab 5

FIG E
Strip Unit 3 – make 1

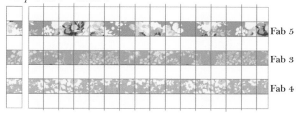

Fab 5
Fab 3
Fab 4

FIG F
Strip Unit 4 – make 1

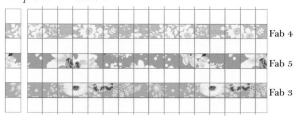

Fab 4
Fab 5
Fab 3

10 To make square Block 1, sew together four segments of Unit 1 with one segment of Unit 2, Unit 3 and Unit 4 as in **Fig G**. Match seams neatly and press. Check the block is 14½in (36.8cm) square. Make seven blocks like this in total.

FIG G
Block 1 – make 7

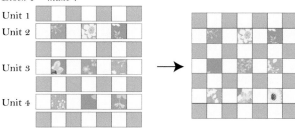

Unit 1
Unit 2
Unit 3
Unit 4

11 To make rectangle Block 2, sew together two segments of Unit 1 with one segment of Unit 2, in the order shown in **Fig H**. Match seams neatly and then press. Check the block is 6½in x 14½in (16.5cm x 36.8cm). Make six blocks like this in total. Set aside until the appliqué has been completed.

FIG H
Block 2 – make 6

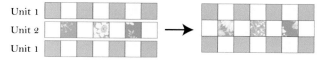

Making the Appliqué Blocks

12 Draw the pattern shapes onto thick coated paper and cut out with sharp scissors. You will need a special fabric glue stick and a thin, hand sewing needle. A pointy wooden stick and tweezers are also useful. Start with a square block. To cut out a fabric shape, place or pin the paper shape on the right side of the fabric and cut out the fabric shape larger than the paper shape, to allow for a seam allowance – allow about ¼in (6mm) for small shapes and about ⅜in (1cm) for larger ones. On very small pieces, make sure the allowance is not too large to be folded around the shape.

13 Now place the paper shape on the wrong side of the fabric, spread glue along the edge of the paper shape (a little at a time) and fold the seam allowance over the shape (**Fig I**). Try not to get glue in the fabric folds, which will make it harder to push the needle through when sewing. With small pieces, it may be easier to press the fabric into place around the edge with a pointy wooden stick or something similar (don't use an iron). If the shape has a lot of curves and angles, snip notches in the edge of the fabric to make folding easier. The fabric edge does not need to be folded over in places where one appliqué will be covered by another.

14 To prepare all the stems and branches, cut about seven ¾in (2cm) wide x width of fabric strips (the curves are gentle so there's no need to cut on the bias). Spread glue over the wrong side of a strip and fold the edges in towards the middle, first one side, then the other (**Fig J**). Prepare all of the appliqués for one block in this way.

FIG I

FIG J

15 Lightly crease a block fabric square into four to mark the centre, to help place the appliqués. Place the prepared appliqués on the fabric square and adjust the positions until you are happy with the layout. Cut the stems to the lengths needed and position under the other appliqués, so the raw ends are covered (**Fig K**). Use a little glue to stick the pieces to the background fabric, or use pins or tacking (basting) stitches.

16 Sew the appliqués to the background fabric with tiny 'invisible' stitches around the edges, matching the sewing thread to the fabric if needed. Try not to sew through the paper shapes.

FIG K
Numbers indicate fabrics used (see Fig A)

17 When all of the shapes are sewn in place remove the paper shapes as follows. From the back of the block cut through the background fabric *only* behind each appliqué and coax out each of the paper pieces (see **Fig L**). Use tweezers to get the small pieces out. Press the work. If the cut-up edges on the back refuse to sit smoothly, glue them to the middle of the appliqué with some glue.

FIG L

18 Repeat this process to sew all of the square blocks. Repeat the process again to prepare the rectangular blocks (see **Fig M** for the layout). When all of the appliqué is finished, trim the blocks to the correct sizes. Trim the square blocks to 14½in (36.8cm) square. Trim the rectangular blocks to 6½in x 14½in (16.5cm x 36.8cm).

FIG M

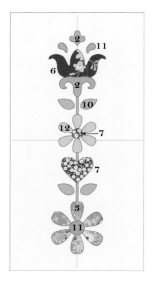

Making the Appliqué Borders

19 The appliqué for the border is worked in the same way as the blocks, using three sizes of flower (sixteen flowers in total) and one large heart. Prepare the appliqués and then lay them out on a border strip, positioning the heart in the centre of the strip (**Fig N** shows the left-hand side). Mirror image the flower positions on the right-hand side of the heart. Glue or pin the shapes into place and sew with tiny stitches, as before. Make two borders like this.

20 When all the border appliqué is finished, press and then trim each border down to 4½in x 54½in (11.4cm x 138.4cm).

Assembling the Quilt

21 Lay out the square blocks, rectangular blocks and appliqué blocks as in **Fig B**. Sew the blocks together in rows, pressing the seams of rows 1, 3 and 5 in one direction and the seams of rows 2 and 4 in the opposite direction. Now sew the rows together and press seams in one direction. Sew the border strips to the top and bottom of the quilt and press seams outwards.

Quilting and Finishing

22 Make a quilt sandwich of the backing fabric, wadding (batting) and quilt. Quilt as desired. Square up the quilt, trimming excess wadding and backing.

23 Use the prepared binding to bind your quilt – see General Techniques: Binding. Add a label to your lovely quilt to finish.

FIG N

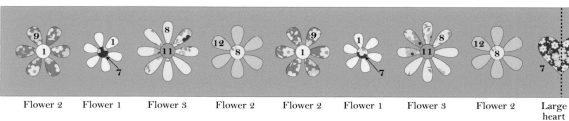

| Flower 2 | Flower 1 | Flower 3 | Flower 2 | Flower 2 | Flower 1 | Flower 3 | Flower 2 | Large heart |

PATCHWORK SQUIRREL

This delightful squirrel is made from pieced squares and is a perfect companion to the next project, a Patchwork Rabbit.

Finished Size 14in x 11in (35.5cm x 28cm)

MATERIALS
- Solid off-white fabric ½yd (50cm)
- Five different patchwork fabrics, 2in x 16½in (5cm x 42cm) strip of each
- Toy stuffing
- Wooden stick
- Tiny amount of black fabric paint for eye
- Label with string (optional)

Making the Squirrel

1 Before you start, refer to the notes in General Techniques: Making Softies. Copy the squirrel pattern pieces from the Patterns section and cut out the shapes. Tape the squirrel parts together on the dashed lines. Fabrics used for the squirrel shown were Solid off-white, Lucille ginger, Tilly dove white, Rabbit and Roses pink, Libby teal and Tess red.

2 The front of the squirrel is made of patchwork squares. The back is solid off-white fabric. To make the patchwork, cut out eight 2in (5cm) squares from one patterned fabric and seven 2in (5cm) squares from each of the other four patterned fabrics, for a total of thirty-six squares. Cut out thirty-six squares from the off-white fabric.

3 Sew the squares together for Row 1 (**Fig A**). Press the seams in one direction. Sew Row 2 together in the same way, but this time press the seams in the opposite direction. Sew the remaining rows, alternating the pressing direction as before. Now sew the rows together as in **Fig B**. Press the long seams open.

FIG A

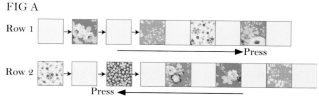

FIG B

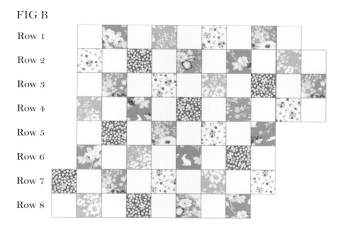

Row 1
Row 2
Row 3
Row 4
Row 5
Row 6
Row 7
Row 8

5 Cut out the squirrel with a seam allowance all round, leaving a little more allowance at the opening. Cut notches in the seam allowance where the edge curves inwards. Turn the figure through using a wooden stick or similar and then press. Stuff using the stick. Don't stuff too firmly – it should be soft, like a cushion. Hand sew up the opening.

6 To finish, stamp on one eye ¼in (6mm–7mm) in diameter on the patchwork side, using a large ball-headed pin and black hobby paint – see General Techniques: Faces. To finish, add a label for a fun detail. Photocopy the label from the Patterns section onto thin card. Punch a hole in the label and use string to tie it around the squirrel's neck.

4 To assemble the squirrel, flip the patchwork over to the wrong side. Flip the pattern too, place it on the patchwork as in **Fig C** and draw the shape. Cut a piece of off-white fabric about 16in x 13in (40.6cm x 33cm) and place it behind the patchwork. Machine sew on the drawn line with a shorter stitch length, about 1.5 (**Fig D**).

FIG C
Flip pattern over and draw on back of patchwork

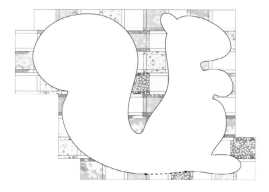

FIG D
Place off-white fabric with patchwork and sew the pattern

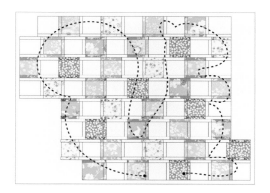

PATCHWORK RABBIT

This rabbit is a little more complicated than the squirrel as it is made from pieced equilateral triangles, rather than squares, but the assembly process is the same.

Finished Size 21¾in x 10½in (55.2cm x 26.7cm)

MATERIALS

- Solid off-white fabric ½yd (50cm)
- Five different patchwork fabrics, 3in x 16½in (7.6cm x 42cm) strip of each
- Toy stuffing
- Wooden stick
- Tiny amount of black fabric paint for eye
- Label with string (optional)

Making the Rabbit

1 Before you start, refer to the notes in General Techniques: Making Softies. Copy the triangle and rabbit patterns from the Patterns section and cut out the shapes. Tape the rabbit parts together on the dashed lines. The triangle template for the patchwork includes a ¼in (6mm) seam allowance, with the dotted line as the seam. Fabrics used for the rabbit shown were Solid off-white, Lucille ginger, Lucille teal, Tess ginger, Tess red and Rabbit and Roses pink.

2 The front of the rabbit is made of patchwork triangles. The back is solid off-white fabric. To make the patchwork, use the template to cut eight triangles from one patterned fabric and seven triangles from each of the other four patterned fabrics, for a total of thirty-six triangles. Cut out thirty-six triangles from off-white fabric. The easiest way to cut the triangles is to cut two strips of fabric 2⅞in (7.3cm) high and rotate the triangle alternately along each strip.

3 The triangles need to be sewn together in rows. If you have a ¼in presser foot, use it; if not, sew ¼in (6mm) inside the edge of the fabric. Start by placing one patterned and one solid triangle right sides together and sew together. Press the seam open. Cut off the excess little triangle (dog ear) where the next triangle will be sewn on. Sew on the next triangle. Follow the sequence shown in **Fig A**. When a row is finished trim off dog ears at the top and bottom.

FIG A

4 Now sew the rows together, starting with Row 1 and Row 2 as in **Fig B**. Place the first row over the second row so they are right sides facing and the triangle tops are against one another. Sew the rows together and press the seam open. Continue adding each of the six rows, noting that there are different numbers of triangles in each row and that the rows are staggered – follow the layout in **Fig C**.

FIG B

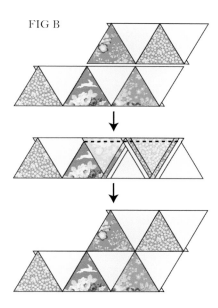

FIG C

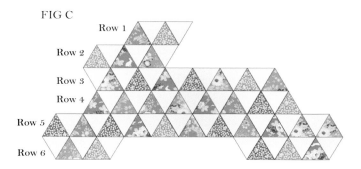

5 To assemble the rabbit, flip the patchwork over to the wrong side. Flip the pattern too, place it on the patchwork as in **Fig D** and draw the shape. Cut a piece of off-white fabric about 24in x 12in (61cm x 30.5cm) and place it behind the patchwork (so they are right sides together). Machine sew on the drawn line with a shorter stitch length, about 1.5 (**Fig E**).

FIG D
Flip pattern over and draw on back of patchwork

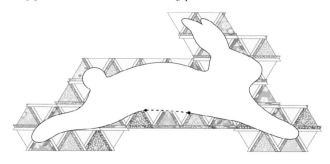

FIG E
Place off-white fabric with patchwork and sew the pattern

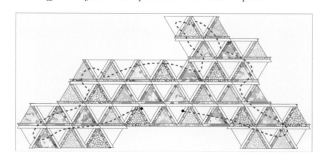

6 Cut out the rabbit with a seam allowance all round, leaving a little more allowance at the opening. Cut notches in the seam allowance where the edge curves inwards. Turn the figure through using a wooden stick or similar and then press. Stuff using the stick. Don't stuff too firmly – it should be soft, like a cushion. Hand sew up the opening.

7 To finish, stamp on one eye ¼in (6mm–7mm) in diameter on the patchwork side, using a large ball-headed pin and black hobby paint – see General Techniques: Faces. To finish you could add a label for a fun detail. Photocopy the label from the Pattern section onto thin card. Punch a hole in the label and use string to tie it around the rabbit's neck.

BIRDS AND SUNFLOWERS QUILT

This gorgeous quilt has four different types of blocks, assembled into vertical columns to create beautiful sunflowers. The Bird blocks in the quilt use curved seams, so are a challenge but the result is well worth the effort. The quilt uses fabrics from various Tilda collections.

Finished Size 50in x 76in (127cm x 193cm)

FIG A
Fabric swatches
If you can't get hold of one or more of these fabrics, just replace with fabrics in similar colours

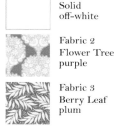
Fabric 1
Solid
off-white

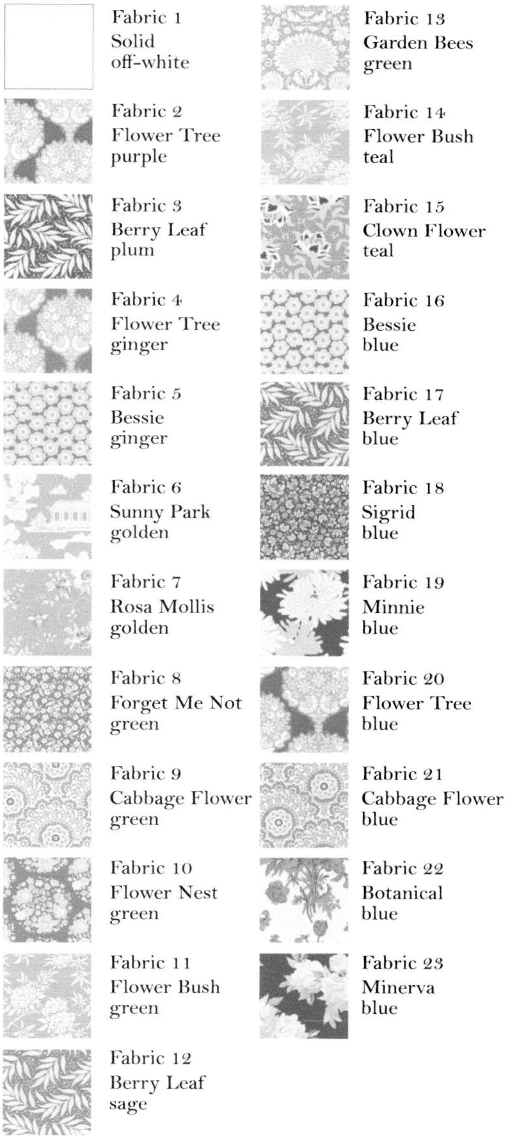

Fabric 2
Flower Tree
purple

Fabric 3
Berry Leaf
plum

Fabric 4
Flower Tree
ginger

Fabric 5
Bessie
ginger

Fabric 6
Sunny Park
golden

Fabric 7
Rosa Mollis
golden

Fabric 8
Forget Me Not
green

Fabric 9
Cabbage Flower
green

Fabric 10
Flower Nest
green

Fabric 11
Flower Bush
green

Fabric 12
Berry Leaf
sage

Fabric 13
Garden Bees
green

Fabric 14
Flower Bush
teal

Fabric 15
Clown Flower
teal

Fabric 16
Bessie
blue

Fabric 17
Berry Leaf
blue

Fabric 18
Sigrid
blue

Fabric 19
Minnie
blue

Fabric 20
Flower Tree
blue

Fabric 21
Cabbage Flower
blue

Fabric 22
Botanical
blue

Fabric 23
Minerva
blue

MATERIALS
- Fabric 1: 3½yd (3.2m) – Solid off-white
- Fabric 2: ¼yd (25cm) – Flower Tree purple
- Fabric 3: ¼yd (25cm) – Berry Leaf plum
- Fabric 4: ¼yd (25cm) – Flower Tree ginger
- Fabric 5: ¼yd (25cm) – Bessie ginger
- Fabric 6: ¼yd (25cm) – Sunny Park golden
- Fabric 7: ¼yd (25cm) – Rosa Mollis golden
- Fabric 8: ⅛yd (15cm) – Forget Me Not green
- Fabric 9: ⅛yd (15cm) – Cabbage Flower green
- Fabric 10: ⅛yd (15cm) – Flower Nest green
- Fabric 11: ⅛yd (15cm) – Flower Bush green
- Fabric 12: ⅛yd (15cm) – Berry Leaf sage
- Fabric 13: ⅛yd (15cm) – Garden Bees green
- Fabric 14: ¼yd (25cm) – Flower Bush teal
- Fabric 15: ¼yd (25cm) – Clown Flower teal
- Fabric 16: ¼yd (25cm) – Bessie blue
- Fabric 17: ¼yd (25cm) – Berry Leaf blue
- Fabric 18: ¼yd (25cm) – Sigrid blue
- Fabric 19: ¼yd (25cm) – Minnie blue
- Fabric 20: ¼yd (25cm) – Flower Tree blue
- Fabric 21: ¼yd (25cm) – Cabbage Flower blue
- Fabric 22: ¼yd (25cm) – Botanical blue
- Fabric 23: ¼yd (25cm) – Minerva blue
- Ten ½in (15mm) buttons for bird eyes
- Backing fabric 3¼yd (3.5m) of standard width
- Wadding (batting) 58in x 84in (147.3cm x 213.4cm)
- Binding fabric – from multiple fabrics (see instructions)
- Template plastic or thin card to make templates

Preparation and Cutting Out

1 Before you start, refer to General Techniques: Making Quilts and Pillows. The quilt is made up of three different Flower blocks (ten in total), six different Bird blocks (ten in total), three different Stem blocks (five in total) and three different Sashing blocks (fifteen in total). An extra border made up of squares, is added at the top and bottom of the quilt. The fabrics used for the quilt are shown in **Fig A** and the quilt layout in **Fig B**.

FIG B
Quilt layout

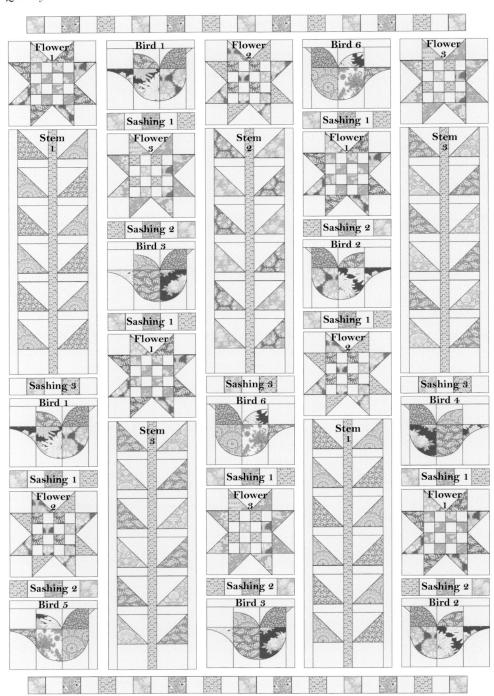

2 Templates are used to create the curved units in the Bird blocks. Note that five Bird blocks face right and five face left. Use template plastic or thin card to create the templates, using the patterns provided in the Patterns section.

3 The specific cutting instructions are given for the four different blocks of the quilt, as it will be simpler to cut the fabrics and make the different blocks as you go along.

4 From the backing fabric cut two pieces 58in (147.3cm) x width of fabric. Remove selvedges, sew the pieces together along the long side and press open. You should have a piece about 58in x 84in (147.3cm x 213.4cm).

5 The binding is a scrappy one. Cut one strip 2½in (6.4cm) x width of fabric from each of the following seven fabrics: 17, 18, 19, 20, 21, 22 and 23. Arrange the fabric strips in this order. Sew the strips together end to end using straight seams and then press seams open. Press the binding in half along the length, wrong sides together.

Making the Flower Blocks

6 The Flower blocks are an eight-point star design and are all made the same way but with three different colourways (Flower 1, Flower 2 and Flower 3). Each block is made up of a centre with sixteen small squares, surrounded by four flying geese units and four plain squares. **Fig C** shows the different fabrics used in the blocks. Cutting and piecing instructions are given for Flower 1, as follows.

FIG C

Flower 1 – make 4

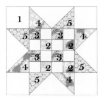
Flower 2 – make 3

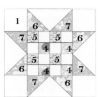
Flower 3 – make 3

7 For one Flower 1 block cut the following.
- Eight 1¾in (4.4cm) squares of Fabric 1.
- Four 1¾in (4.4cm) squares of Fabric 6.
- Four 1¾in (4.4cm) squares of Fabric 7.
- Four 3in (7.6cm) squares of Fabric 1.
- Four 5½in x 3in (14cm x 7.6cm) rectangles of Fabric 1, for flying geese.
- Four 3in (7.6cm) squares of Fabric 2, for flying geese.
- Four 3in (7.6cm) squares of Fabric 3, for flying geese.

8 Sew the sixteen 1¾in (4.4cm) squares together as in **Fig D**, alternating the off-white with the print fabrics as shown. Press and check the unit is 5½in (14cm) square.

9 Using one 5½in x 3in (14cm x 7.6cm) Fabric 1 rectangle, one 3in square of Fabric 2 and one 3in square of Fabric 3, make a flying geese unit as described in General Techniques: Flying Geese – Single Unit. Press and check the unit is 5½in x 3in (14cm x 7.6cm). Make four units like this in total.

10 Lay out the units for one Flower block as in **Fig D**. Sew the units together in rows and then sew the rows together. Press and check the block is 10½in (26.7cm) square. Make four Flower 1 blocks like this in total.

FIG D

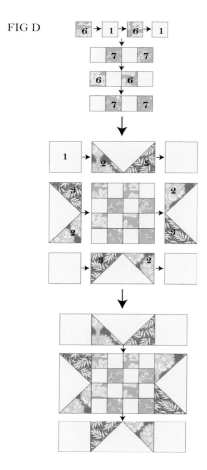

11 Use the same techniques and the fabrics shown in **Fig C** to make three Flower 2 blocks. For one Flower 2 block cut the following.
- Eight 1¾in (4.4cm) squares of Fabric 1.
- Four 1¾in (4.4cm) squares of Fabric 3.
- Four 1¾in (4.4cm) squares of Fabric 2.
- Four 3in (7.6cm) squares of Fabric 1.
- Four 5½in x 3in (14cm x 7.6cm) rectangles of Fabric 1, for flying geese.
- Four 3in (7.6cm) squares of Fabric 4, for flying geese.
- Four 3in (7.6cm) squares of Fabric 5, for flying geese.

12 Use the same techniques and the fabrics shown in **Fig C** to make three Flower 3 blocks. For one Flower 3 block cut the following.
- Eight 1¾in (4.4cm) squares of Fabric 1.
- Four 1¾in (4.4cm) squares of Fabric 5.
- Four 1¾in (4.4cm) squares of Fabric 4.

- Four 3in (7.6cm) squares of Fabric 1.
- Four 5½in x 3in (14cm x 7.6cm) rectangles of Fabric 1, for flying geese.
- Four 3in (7.6cm) squares of Fabric 6, for flying geese.
- Four 3in (7.6cm) squares of Fabric 7, for flying geese.

Making the Stem Blocks

13 The Stem blocks are all made the same way but with three different colourways (Stem 1, Stem 2 and Stem 3). Each block is made up of twelve half-square triangle (HST) units and two plain rectangles, separated by short strips and long strips. **Fig E** shows the different fabrics used in the blocks. Cutting and piecing instructions are given for Stem 1. The HST units are made using a two at once method.

FIG E

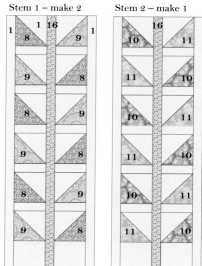
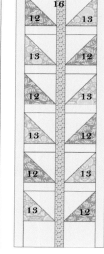

Stem 1 – make 2   Stem 2 – make 1   Stem 3 – make 2

14 For one Stem 1 block cut the following.
- Six 4½in (11.4cm) squares of Fabric 1, for HSTs.
- Three 4½in (11.4cm) squares of Fabric 8, for HSTs.
- Three 4½in (11.4cm) squares of Fabric 9, for HSTs.
- Ten 1½in x 4in (3.8cm x 10.2cm) rectangles of Fabric 1.
- Two 4in x 3½in (10.2cm x 7.6cm) rectangles of Fabric 1.
- One 1½in x 29½in (3.8cm x 75cm) strip of Fabric 16.
- Two 1½in x 29½in (3.8cm x 75cm) strips of Fabric 1.

15 Make six HST units using Fabric 1 and Fabric 8, and six HST units using Fabric 1 and Fabric 9, following the method in General Techniques: Half-Square Triangles – Two at Once. Press each unit and trim it to 4in (10.2cm) square.

16 Lay out the units for one Stem block as in **Fig F**. Sew the units together in columns. Press and check the block is 10½in x 29½in (26.7cm x 75cm). Make one more Stem 1 block like this.

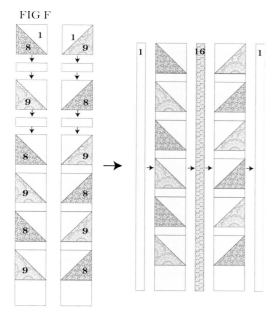

FIG F

17 Use the same techniques and the fabrics shown in **Fig E** to make one Stem 2 block. For one Stem 2 block cut the same pieces as Stem block 1 but use 4½in (11.4cm) squares of Fabric 10 and Fabric 11 for the HSTs.

18 Use the same techniques and the fabrics shown in **Fig E** to make two Stem 3 blocks. For one Stem 3 block cut the same pieces as Stem block 1 but use 4½in (11.4cm) squares of Fabric 12 and Fabric 13 for the HSTs.

Making the Sashing Blocks

19 The Sashing blocks are all made the same way but with three different colourways (Sashing 1, Sashing 2 and Sashing 3). Each block is made up of five 2½in (6.4cm) squares. **Fig G** shows the placement of the fabrics and also the number of each unit to make. Sew the squares together as shown and press. Check each sewn unit is 2½in x 10½in (6.4cm x 26.7cm).

20 For one Sashing 1 block cut the following.
• Two 2½in (6.4cm) squares Fabric 1.
• One 2½in (6.4cm) square each of Fabric 14, 15 and 16.

21 For one Sashing 2 block cut the following.
• Two 2½in (6.4cm) squares Fabric 1.
• One 2½in (6.4cm) square each of Fabric 16, 15 and 14.

22 For one Sashing 3 block cut the following.
• Three 2½in (6.4cm) squares Fabric 1.
• One 2½in (6.4cm) square each of Fabric 14 and 16.

Sashing 1 – make 7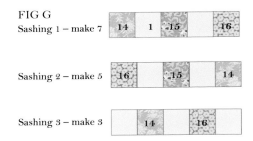

Sashing 2 – make 5

Sashing 3 – make 3

Making the Bird Blocks

23 The Bird blocks are all made the same way but with different colourways. Each block is made up of eight different units and five of these use curved seams. Bird 2 is a mirror image of Bird 1, Bird 4 is a mirror image of Bird 3 and Bird 6 is a mirror image of Bird 5. So the templates used for the curved shapes in Blocks 2, 4 and 6 will need to be reversed (flipped) before you use them. The templates already include a ¼in (6mm) seam allowance. **Fig H** shows the fabrics used for the different blocks and the number of each block you need to make.

FIG H

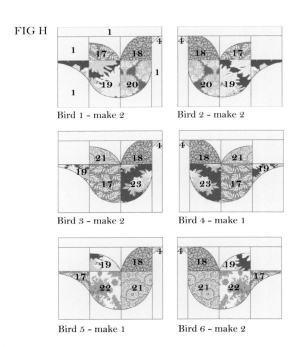

Bird 1 - make 2   Bird 2 - make 2

Bird 3 - make 2   Bird 4 - make 1

Bird 5 - make 1   Bird 6 - make 2

24 The various units of a Bird block are given a number (**Fig I**) so select the correct patterns. For Unit 1 use patterns 1A and 1B, for Unit 2 use patterns 2A and 2B, and so on. Cut your fabric pieces a little bigger than the patterns. Draw the shapes carefully on the correct fabrics and cut them out (**Fig J**). If you place the straight edges of a pattern piece on the straight edges of the fabric piece you won't need to mark all around the shape (see also the Tip).

> **TIP** The back of a fabric is usually lighter than the right side, so if you want to mark the pattern on the back of a fabric then remember to flip the pattern over before you draw round it, so the cut piece will be the right way round.

FIG I

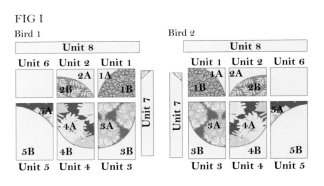

FIG J

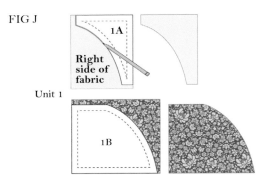

25 Curved seams can be tricky so take your time. The piecing of Unit 1 is shown in **Fig K**. Place the A and B pieces right sides together, aligning the bottom right corners, and pin. Begin to align the curves of the pieces, placing more pins and keeping the curve smooth, easing to fit. Sew the seam ¼in (6mm) from the edge of the curve. Remove the pins, clip into the seam allowance in a few places and press the seam outwards.

FIG K

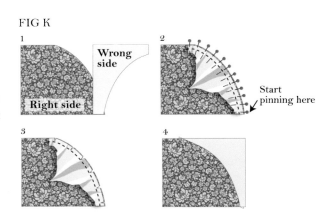

26 Follow this process to sew the other curved units. Once sewn and pressed, check the units are the correct sizes.
- Unit 1: 3½in x 3in (8.9cm x 7.6cm).
- Unit 2: 3½in x 3in (8.9cm x 7.6cm).
- Unit 3: 3½in x 5½in (8.9cm x 14cm).
- Unit 4: 3½in x 5½in (8.9cm x 14cm).
- Unit 5: 3½in x 5½in (8.9cm x 14cm).
- Unit 6: cut a Fabric 1 piece 3½in x 3in (8.9cm x 7.6cm).
- Unit 7: see the next step for making this unit.
- Unit 8: cut a Fabric 1 piece 10½in x 1½in (26.7cm x 3.8cm).

27 To make Unit 7, which has the bird's beak, cut a Fabric 1 piece 1½in x 8in (3.8cm x 20.3cm) and a Fabric 4 piece 1¼in (3.2cm) square. Place the square right sides together on the off-white strip as in **Fig L** (for Bird blocks 1, 3 and 5) and sew across the diagonal. Trim excess fabric ¼in (6mm) from the sewn line. Press the triangle into place. (Remember when making Bird blocks 2, 4 and 6 that the triangle needs to face the *opposite* way, so place it in the top right corner before sewing.)

FIG L
Unit 7 for Bird blocks 1, 3 and 5

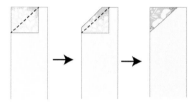

28 Take the eight units for a Bird block and sew them together as in **Fig M**, matching seams where needed. Press and check the block is 10½in x 9in (26.7cm x 22.9cm).

FIG M

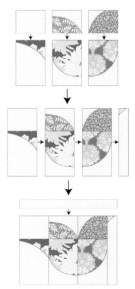

29 Use the same process to make the remaining Bird 1, Bird 3 and Bird 5 blocks (see **Fig H**). Use the same process to make the Bird 2, Bird 4 and Bird 6 blocks, remembering to flip the templates over, so you cut *reversed* pieces – see Bird 2 in **Fig I**.

Making the Borders

30 There is a border of squares at the top and at the bottom of the quilt. For *each* of these borders cut the following 2½in (6.4cm) squares.
- Twelve squares of Fabric 1.
- Five squares of Fabric 14.
- Four squares of Fabric 15.
- Four squares of Fabric 16.

Sew the squares together in the repeating order shown in **Fig N**. Press the seams open or in one direction. Make two borders like this.

FIG N

Assembling the Quilt

31 Lay out all of the blocks in columns, in the order shown in **Fig B**. Sew the blocks together column by column. Now sew the columns together – note that you do not need to align any seams. Press the long seams open or to one side. Finally, sew the top and bottom borders in place and press. The borders should fit the horizontal measurement of the quilt but ease to fit if need be.

Quilting and Finishing

32 Make a quilt sandwich of the backing fabric, wadding (batting) and quilt. Quilt as desired. Square up the quilt, trimming excess wadding and backing. Sew a button to each bird for an eye.

33 Use the prepared binding to bind your quilt – see General Techniques: Binding. Add a label to your beautiful quilt to finish.

BIRDS AND SUNFLOWERS PILLOWS

*These lovely pillows use blocks from the Birds and Sunflowers Quilt and some of the same fabrics, so refer to the fabric swatches in **Fig A** of the quilt. Instructions and materials are given for the Sunflower Pillow. The Bird Pillow uses three of the Bird blocks from the quilt.*

Finished Sizes
Sunflower pillow: 30in x 23½in (76.2cm x 60cm)
Bird pillow: 30in x 13in (76.2cm x 33cm)

MATERIALS

Sunflower Pillow
- Fabric 1: ¾yd (75cm) – Solid off-white
- Small amounts of various print fabrics
- Wadding (batting) 31in x 25in (79cm x 63.5cm)
- Lining fabric 31in x 25in (79cm x 63.5cm) (optional)
- Fabric for back of cushion, two pieces 24in x 19in (61cm x 48cm)
- Binding fabric ¼yd (25cm) – Fabric 20 (Flower Tree blue)
- Three buttons of your choice for the pillow back

SUNFLOWER PILLOW

1 Follow the Birds and Sunflower Quilt instructions, steps 6–12, to make one block each of Flower 1, Flower 2 and Flower 3. **Fig A** here shows the blocks and fabrics used.

FIG A

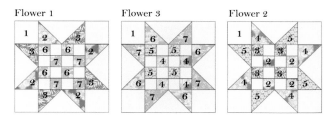

Flower 1   Flower 3   Flower 2

2 Follow the Birds and Sunflower Quilt instructions, steps 13–18, to make one block each of Stem 1, Stem 2 and Stem 3, but note that the blocks here are shorter, so you only need to make six half-square triangle units for each block. The long 1½in (3.8cm) wide strips only need to be 14in (35.5cm) tall for the pillow. **Fig B** here shows these shorter blocks and the fabrics used.

FIG B
Stem 1 – short version   Stem 2 – short version   Stem 3 – short version

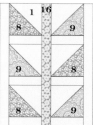 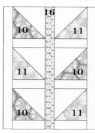 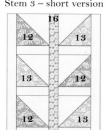

3 Sew the blocks together as shown in **Fig C** here, and press.

FIG C

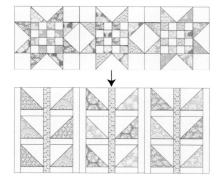

4 Make a quilt sandwich of the patchwork, wadding (batting) and the lining fabric (if using). Quilt as desired.

5 The pillow is assembled with an overlapped back, with buttons to secure. Use the two pieces of fabric for the back and follow the instructions in General Techniques: Button-Fastening Cushion.

6 For the binding, cut three 2½in (6.4cm) x width of fabric strips of Fabric 20. Sew together and prepare as a double-fold binding. Bind the cushion edge to finish (see General Techniques: Binding).

BIRD PILLOW

This pillow features three Bird blocks, bordered by 2½in (6.4cm) squares. Refer to the Birds and Sunflowers Quilt, steps 23–29, for making the Bird 2, Bird 4 and Bird 6 blocks (reverse the patterns before use). Follow **Fig D** here for the blocks and **Fig E** here for the pillow assembly. Once pieced, the patchwork is 30½in x 13in (77.5cm x 33cm). Make a quilt sandwich and quilt as desired. Sew on a button for each bird's eye. Make up the cushion in the same way as the Sunflower Pillow, using fabric pieces suitable for the size of this pillow. For the binding, cut three 2½in (6.4cm) x width of fabric strips of Fabric 4.

FIG D

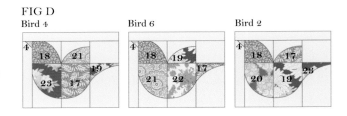

FIG E

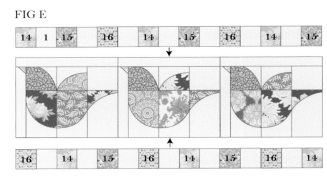

PATCH FOX

These foxes are full of mischief and ready to play. The pattern is given in large and small. Specific fabrics and instructions are given for the small fox but you could just choose any five print fabrics plus the off-white. The fat quarters allowed for the small fox are generous.

Finished Sizes
Large: 30in (76.2cm) tall
Small: 24in (61cm) tall

MATERIALS
- Fabric 1: one fat quarter – Solid off-white
- Fabric 2: one fat quarter – Cabbage Flower purple
- Fabric 3: one fat quarter – Cabbage Flower green
- Fabric 4: one fat quarter – Flower Tree green
- Fabric 5: one fat quarter – Flower Tree ginger
- Fabric 6: one fat quarter – Bessie ginger
- Wooden stick for turning pieces through to the right side and for stuffing
- Toy stuffing
- Black hobby paint for eyes
- Rouge or lipstick and dry brush for cheek blush
- Embroidery cotton (floss) for stitching nose

FIG A
Fabric swatches
If you can't get hold of one or more of these fabrics, just replace with fabrics in similar colours

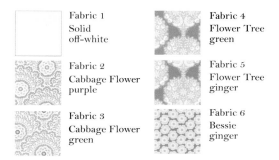

Fabric 1 Solid off–white	**Fabric 4** Flower Tree green
Fabric 2 Cabbage Flower purple	**Fabric 5** Flower Tree ginger
Fabric 3 Cabbage Flower green	**Fabric 6** Bessie ginger

Preparation

1 Before you start, refer to the notes in General Techniques: Making Softies. The fox comes in two sizes, large and small, so copy all the relevant pattern pieces from the Patterns section and cut out the shapes. Some patterns are split to fit the page, so assemble the patterns as needed. **Fig A** shows the fabrics used for the small fox. A second version of the small fox uses Solid off-white, Flower Tree purple, Flower Tree blue, Bessie purple, Cabbage Flower green, Flower Bush teal.

The large fox uses a fat quarter each of the following fabrics: Solid off-white, Flower Tree blue, Flower Tree purple, Bessie blue, Cabbage Flower blue, Cabbage Flower purple. If making the large fox, remember to increase the sizes of the fabric pieces you cut, to fit the larger patterns.

Making the Fox

2 Head: For the face, fold the off-white fabric in half, right sides facing. Mark and cut out two mirrored shapes with a seam allowance all round. Mark the small lines on the fabric edge. For the head front and head back pieces, cut a piece of Fabric 5 and Fabric 6 each 14in x 9¼in (35.5cm x 23.5cm) and place the fabrics right sides together with Fabric 5 on top. Mark and cut out with a seam allowance all round.

3 Sewing each side of the head in turn, pin an off-white face piece right sides together with a Fabric 5 head front piece, matching up the small marks first and then easing the rest of the curves to fit together (**Fig B1**). Sew the curved seam and press the seam open. Repeat with the other side of the face (**Fig B2**). Sew the two front head pieces together, down along the nose and along the chin (**Fig B3**).

FIG B

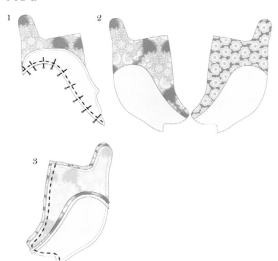

4 Pin the two head back pieces right sides together and sew down the centre join, leaving a gap where shown on the pattern (**Fig C1**). Pin the head front and head back pieces together, matching seams, and sew all around the edge (**Fig C2**). Turn through to the right side and press. Stuff the head and sew up the gap.

FIG C

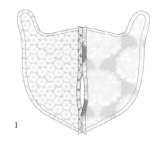 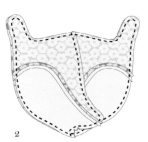

5 Arms and Legs: The arms and legs are cut out from pieced fabrics, so the paws and feet are in a different fabric to the main arm and leg pieces. The fabric order is reversed on the back of the limbs. From Fabric 3 and Fabric 4 cut a piece about 14in x 10in (35.5cm x 25.5cm). From Fabric 2 and Fabric 5 cut a piece about 14in x 4½in (35.5cm x 11.4cm). Sew the larger piece of Fabric 4 to the smaller piece of Fabric 2 and press. Sew the larger piece of Fabric 3 to the smaller piece of Fabric 5 (**Fig D1**).

6 Place the Fabric 4+2 piece right side down on the Fabric 5+3 piece, aligning the sewn seams. Draw around the leg and arm patterns (**Fig D2**), placing the dashed line of the paw/foot horizontally on the seamline. Allow space around each pattern for a seam allowance. Sew and then cut out each shape with a seam allowance. Turn the limbs through to the right side and stuff.

FIG D

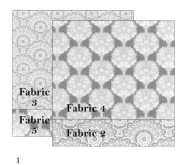 

7 Body: The patchwork body is created in a similar way to the limbs, except only two pieces of fabric are needed as the front and back are the same fabric. From Fabric 2 cut a piece about 14in x 7½in (35.5cm x 19cm). From Fabric 6 cut a piece about 14in x 6½in (35.5cm x 16.5cm). Sew the pieces together and press open. Fold in half, right sides together. Mark the pattern, placing the dashed line of the pattern on the seamline. Sew along the marked lines (**Fig E1**). Cut out with a seam allowance all round (**Fig E2**). Turn up and press the hem at the bottom of the body (**Fig E3**). Keep wrong side out and don't stuff yet.

FIG E

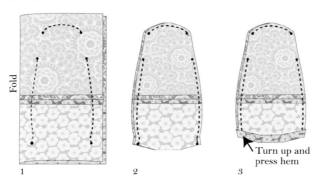

8 Tail: The tail is made in the same way as the body. Cut a piece of Fabric 5 about 14in x 6¾in (35.5cm x 17cm) for the tail upper, and a piece of Fabric 6 about 14in x 4½in (35.5cm x 11.4cm) for the tail tip. Sew the Fabric 5 piece to the top of Fabric 6. Press the seam open. Fold the pieced fabric in half vertically, right sides together. Mark the tail pattern, sew and cut out with a seam allowance. Turn through to the right side, press and stuff.

Assembly

9 Place the stuffed arms inside the body and sew securely in place (**Fig F1**). Turn the body through to the right side and stuff. Before closing the bottom seam, pin the legs in position towards the sides of the gap and pin the tail in the centre of the opening. Hand sew securely into place (**Fig F2**).

FIG F

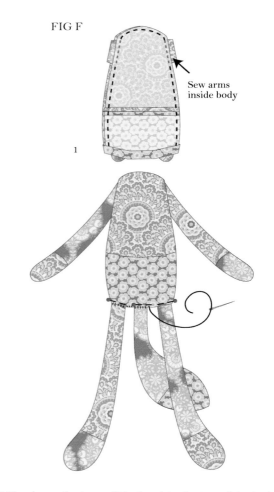

Sew arms inside body

10 Hand sew the base of the head to the top of the body – the head is meant to be dangly. To make the face, use black hobby paint, a little lipstick or rouge and a dry brush. Stamp on the eyes ¼in (6mm–7mm) in diameter, using a large ball-headed pin and black hobby paint – see General Techniques: Faces. Once the eyes are dry, mark rosy cheeks with lipstick or rouge and a dry brush. Finally, satin stitch the nose with the embroidery thread (Fig G).

FIG G

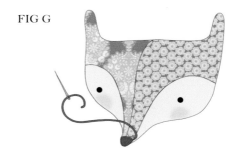

PUMPKIN HARVEST QUILT

Celebrate the season with this fun quilt on a pumpkin theme. The curved look of the pumpkins is created with simple machine piecing, so no templates are needed. It uses fabrics from the lovely Harvest collection.

Finished Size 74½in x 52½in (189cm x 133.5cm)

FIG A
Fabric swatches
If you can't get hold of one or more of these fabrics, just replace with fabrics in similar colours

Fabric 1
Solid
off-white

Fabric 2
Flower Tree
blue

Fabric 3
Cabbage Flower
blue

Fabric 4
Bessie
blue

Fabric 5
Bird Tree
blue

Fabric 6
Flower Bush
teal

Fabric 7
Bessie
purple

Fabric 8
Autumn Rose
lilac

Fabric 9
Flower Tree
purple

Fabric 10
Bird Tree
purple

Fabric 11
Cabbage Flower
purple

Fabric 12
Bird Tree
green

Fabric 13
Cabbage Flower
green

Fabric 14
Autumn Rose
green

Fabric 15
Flower Tree
green

Fabric 16
Flower Bush
green

Fabric 17
Flower Tree
ginger

Fabric 18
Bird Tree
ginger

Fabric 19
Flower Bush
pink

Fabric 20
Bessie
ginger

Fabric 21
Autumn Rose
ginger

MATERIALS

- Fabric 1: 2yd (1.9m) – Solid off-white
- Fabric 2: ⅜yd (40cm) – Flower Tree blue
- Fabric 3: ⅛yd (15cm) – Cabbage Flower blue
- Fabric 4: ¼yd (25cm) – Bessie blue
- Fabric 5: ¼yd (25cm) – Bird Tree blue
- Fabric 6: ¼yd (25cm) – Flower Bush teal
- Fabric 7: ¼yd (25cm) – Bessie purple
- Fabric 8: ¼yd (25cm) – Autumn Rose lilac
- Fabric 9: ¼yd (25cm) – Flower Tree purple
- Fabric 10: ¼yd (25cm) – Bird Tree purple
- Fabric 11: ¼yd (25cm) – Cabbage Flower purple
- Fabric 12: ¼yd (25cm) – Bird Tree green
- Fabric 13: ¼yd (25cm) – Cabbage Flower green
- Fabric 14: ¼yd (25cm) – Autumn Rose green
- Fabric 15: ⅜yd (40cm) – Flower Tree green
- Fabric 16: ¼yd (25cm) – Flower Bush green
- Fabric 17: ¼yd (25cm) – Flower Tree ginger
- Fabric 18: ⅛yd (15cm) – Bird Tree ginger
- Fabric 19: ⅜yd (40cm) – Flower Bush pink
- Fabric 20: ⅜yd (40cm) – Bessie ginger
- Fabric 21: ¼yd (25cm) – Autumn Rose ginger
- Backing fabric 3½yd (3.25m) of standard width
- Wadding (batting) 61in x 83in (155cm x 211cm)
- Binding fabric – from multiple fabrics (see instructions)

Preparation and Cutting Out

1 There are thirty-two pumpkin blocks in the quilt in a 4 x 8 block layout. There are four different colourways for the blocks. The blocks are separated by narrow sashing strips. The fabrics used for the quilt are shown in **Fig A** and the quilt layout in **Fig B**.

TIP If you want to have the long horizontal sashing strips without seams, then cut all the sashing strips first from the length of the off-white fabric. Cut the rest of the pieces from the remaining width or length.

FIG B
Quilt layout

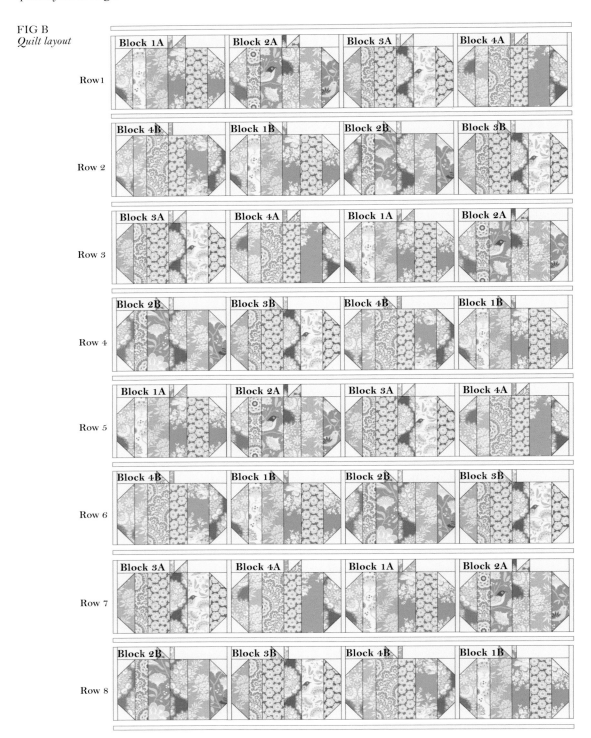

Row 1 — Block 1A, Block 2A, Block 3A, Block 4A

Row 2 — Block 4B, Block 1B, Block 2B, Block 3B

Row 3 — Block 3A, Block 4A, Block 1A, Block 2A

Row 4 — Block 2B, Block 3B, Block 4B, Block 1B

Row 5 — Block 1A, Block 2A, Block 3A, Block 4A

Row 6 — Block 4B, Block 1B, Block 2B, Block 3B

Row 7 — Block 3A, Block 4A, Block 1A, Block 2A

Row 8 — Block 2B, Block 3B, Block 4B, Block 1B

2 From Fabric 1 cut ten 2in (5cm) x width of fabric strips for the tops of the pumpkin blocks. Sub-cut these as follows.
- Thirty-two 2in x 6½in (5cm x 16.5cm).
- Thirty-two 2in x 5in (5cm x 12.7cm).

3 From Fabric 1 cut one 2½in (6.4cm) x width of fabric strip for half-square triangles in the tops of the pumpkin blocks. Sub-cut these into sixteen 2½in (6.4cm) squares.

4 From Fabric 1 cut eight 2½in (6.4cm) x width of fabric strips for the triangle corners. Sub-cut these into 128 squares 2½in (6.4cm).

5 From Fabric 1 cut sashing strips as follows.
- Forty 1in x 9¼in (2.5cm x 23.5cm) for short vertical sashing.
- Nine 1in x 53in (2.5cm x 134.6cm) for long horizontal sashing, joining strips as necessary if cutting across the fabric width.

6 From Fabric 2 cut the following.
- Sixteen 2½in x 7¾in (6.4cm x 19.7cm) for blocks.
- Eight 1in x 2in (2.5cm x 5cm) for stalks.

7 From each of Fabric 3 and Fabric 18 cut eight 2in x 7¾in (5cm x 19.7cm) for blocks.

8 From each of Fabric 4, Fabric 5, Fabric 7, Fabric 8, Fabric 17 and Fabric 21 cut eight 2½in x 7¾in (6.4cm x 19.7cm) for blocks. Cut sixteen from Fabric 15.

9 From Fabric 6 cut the following.
- Eight 2in x 7¾in (5cm x 19.7cm) for blocks.
- Four 2½in (6.4cm) squares for half-square triangles.

10 From Fabric 9 cut the following.
- Eight 2½in x 7¾in (6.4cm x 19.7cm) for blocks.
- Eight 1in x 2in (2.5cm x 5cm) for stalks.

11 From each of Fabric 10, Fabric 13 and Fabric 14 cut eight pieces 3in x 7¾in (7.6cm x 19.7cm) for blocks.

12 From Fabric 11 cut the following.
- Eight 2in x 7¾in (5cm x 19.7cm) for blocks.
- Four 2½in (6.4cm) squares for half-square triangles.

13 From Fabric 12 cut the following.
- Eight 3in x 7¾in (7.6cm x 19.7cm) for blocks.
- Eight 1in x 2in (2.5cm x 5cm) for stalks.

14 From Fabric 16 cut the following.
- Eight 3in x 7¾in (7.6cm x 19.7cm) for blocks.
- Four 2½in (6.4cm) squares for half-square triangles.

15 From Fabric 19 cut the following.
- Eight 3in x 7¾in (7.6cm x 19.7cm) for blocks.
- Eight 2½in x 7¾in (6.4cm x 19.7cm) for blocks.
- Eight 1in x 2in (2.5cm x 5cm) for stalks.

16 From Fabric 20 cut the following.
- Sixteen 3in x 7¾in (7.6cm x 19.7cm) for blocks.
- Four 2½in (6.4cm) squares for half-square triangles.

17 From the backing fabric cut two pieces 61in (155cm) x width of fabric. Remove the selvedges, sew the pieces together along the long side and press the seam open. Trim to approximately 61in x 83in (155cm x 211cm).

18 The binding is a scrappy one. Cut one strip 2½in x 18¼in (6.4cm x 46.4cm) from each of the following fabrics: 2, 20, 8, 6, 19, 15, 3, 17, 16, 7, 21, 9, 4, 11 and 14. Sew the strips together end to end in this order using straight seams and press seams open. Press the binding in half along the length, wrong sides together.

Making a Block

19 All of the pumpkin bodies are made in the same way, with six strips of different fabrics of varying widths – **Fig C** shows Block 1 as an example, with the strip measurements. The curved appearance of the body is created with triangle corners of off-white fabric. The pumpkin tops are all made using the same method but half of them have the leaf facing the opposite way. There are four different colourways for the quilt blocks. Instructions are given here for making Block 1.

20 To make the pumpkin base, follow **Fig C**, laying out the fabric strips side by side and following sizes given and fabric order. Sew the strips together and press the seams.

FIG C

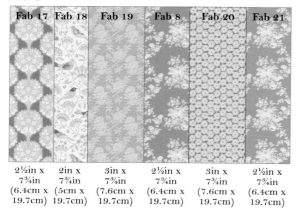

2½in x 7¾in (6.4cm x 19.7cm) 2in x 7¾in (5cm x 19.7cm) 3in x 7¾in (7.6cm x 19.7cm) 2½in x 7¾in (6.4cm x 19.7cm) 3in x 7¾in (7.6cm x 19.7cm) 2½in x 7¾in (6.4cm x 19.7cm)

21 To create the corner triangles, take four 2½in (6.4cm) squares of off-white fabric and mark a diagonal line from corner to corner on the wrong side of the fabric (note: there is no right or wrong side to the solid fabric). Place the squares right side down in each corner of the pumpkin base patchwork, with the marked lines as in **Fig D**. Sew along each marked line and then trim off the excess corner ¼in (6mm) from the marked line. Press the corners outwards.

FIG D

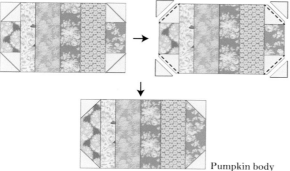

Pumpkin body

22 To make the pumpkin top, start by making half-square triangle (HST) units, using a 2½in (6.4cm) off-white square and a print square (for Block 1 this is Fabric 16). Refer to General Techniques: Half-Square Triangles – Two at Once. Trim each HST unit to 2in (5cm) square.

23 To assemble the pumpkin top (for Block 1), **Fig E** shows the size of the pieces needed and the fabrics used.
- One 6½in x 2in (16.5cm x 5cm) piece of off-white fabric.
- One 1in x 2in (2.5cm x 5cm) piece of Fabric 12.
- One 2in (5cm) HST of off-white/Fabric 16.
- One 5in x 2in (12.7cm x 5cm) piece of off-white fabric.

Place the pieces in a row, sew them together and press. This is pumpkin top A.

FIG E
Pumpkin top A

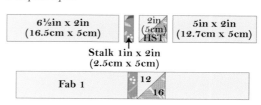

24 For half of the blocks in the quilt, the pumpkin top is reversed, so the leaf faces the other way. This is pumpkin top B. Make it in the same way as before but follow the position of the pieces shown in **Fig F**.

FIG F
Pumpkin top B

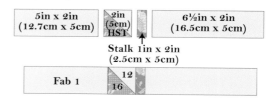

25 Take a Block 1 pumpkin body and sew it to a pumpkin top A as in **Fig G** and press. This is now Block 1A. Check it is 9¼in x 13in (23.5cm x 33cm).

FIG G

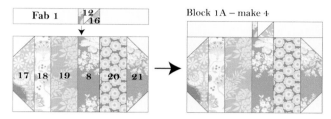

26 Make the rest of the blocks using the same process. **Fig H** gives details of the specific fabrics and shows whether pumpkin top A or B is needed. Note that the HST units are made from different prints in each of the four block types. You need to make four of each of the following blocks: 1A, 1B, 2A, 2B, 3A, 3B, 4A and 4B.

FIG H

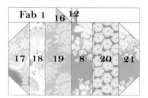

Block 1B – make 4

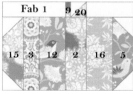

Block 2A – make 4   Block 2B – make 4

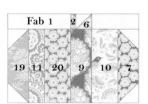

Block 3A – make 4   Block 3B – make 4

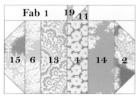

Block 4A – make 4   Block 4B – make 4

Assembling the Quilt

27 Lay out the blocks in the order shown in **Fig B**. Working on Row 1, sew the blocks together with a 1in x 9¼in (2.5cm x 23.5cm) strip of off-white sashing between each block and at each end of the row, as in **Fig I**. Press the seams. Repeat this process using the blocks for Row 2 and five more sashing strips (**Fig J**). Continue in this way to sew all of the rows.

FIG I
Row 1

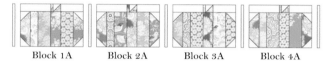

Block 1A   Block 2A   Block 3A   Block 4A

FIG J
Row 2

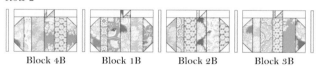

Block 4B   Block 1B   Block 2B   Block 3B

28 Sew the rows together, adding a 1in x 53in (2.5cm x 134.6cm) sashing strip between each row and at the top and bottom of the quilt. Press long seams open or to one side.

Quilting and Finishing

29 Make a quilt sandwich of the backing fabric, wadding (batting) and quilt. Quilt as desired. Square up the quilt, trimming excess wadding and backing.

30 Use the prepared binding to bind your quilt – see General Techniques: Binding. Add a label to your gorgeous quilt to finish.

HARVEST PILLOW

*This pillow is like an old-fashioned but ultra-comfy bolster pillow. It features three of the blocks from the Pumpkin Harvest Quilt and uses some of the same fabrics, so refer to the fabric swatches in **Fig A** of the quilt.*

Finished Size 11¾in x 40in (30cm x 101.5cm)

MATERIALS

- Fabric 1: ⅜yd (40cm) – Solid off-white
- Small pieces of the print fabrics (except Fabrics 3 and 5) – maximum of 6in x 8in (15.2cm x 20.3cm) of each
- Wadding (batting) 14in x 42in (35.5cm x 107cm)
- Lining fabric 14in x 42in (35.5cm x 107cm) (optional)
- Fabric for back of cushion, two pieces 11¾in x 25in (30cm x 63.5cm)
- Binding fabric – from multiple fabrics (see instructions)
- Three buttons for pillow back

Making the Pillow

1 From Fabric 1 cut the following pieces.
- Three 5in x 2in (12.7cm x 5cm).
- Three 6½in x 2in (16.5cm x 5cm).
- Three 2½in (6.4cm) squares for half-square triangles.
- Twelve 2½in (6.4cm) squares for block corners.
- Four 1in x 9¼in (2.5cm x 23.5cm) for vertical sashing.
- One 1½in x 40in (3.8cm x 101.6cm) for top border.
- One 2in x 40in (5cm x 101.6cm) for bottom border.

2 From Fabrics 2, 4, 7, 8, 9, 15, 17, 19 and 21, cut a piece 2½in x 7¾in (6.4cm x 19.7cm).

3 From Fabrics 6, 11 and 18, cut a piece 2in x 7¾in (5cm x 19.7cm).

4 From Fabrics 10, 13, 14 and 19, cut one piece 3in x 7¾in (7.6cm x 19.7cm). From Fabric 20 cut two pieces.

5 From Fabrics 2, 12 and 19, cut a piece 1in x 2in (2.5cm x 5cm) for stalks.

6 From Fabrics 6, 11 and 16, cut a 2½in (6.4cm) square for half-square triangle units.

7 For the binding, cut one strip 2½in x 7¾in (6.4cm x 19.7cm) from Fabrics 2, 20, 8, 6, 19, 15, 3, 17, 16, 7, 21, 9, 4, 11 and 14. Sew together and prepare as a binding.

8 Follow the Pumpkin Harvest Quilt instructions to make the blocks, making one Block 1B, one Block 3B and one Block 4B. **Fig A** here shows the blocks and fabrics used.

FIG A

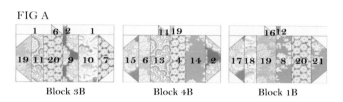

Block 3B   Block 4B   Block 1B

9 Place the blocks in the order shown in **Fig B** here, with short sashing strips between the blocks and at both ends. Sew together and press seams away from the off-white fabric. Add the long narrow sashing strip to the top of the patchwork and the wider piece to the bottom, and press.

FIG B

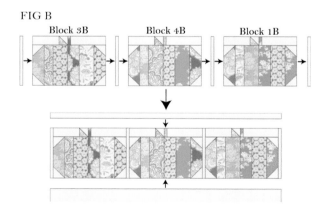

10 Make a quilt sandwich of the patchwork, wadding (batting) and lining fabric (if using). Quilt as desired.

11 The pillow is assembled with an overlapped back, with buttons to secure. Use the two pieces of fabric for the cushion back and follow the instructions in General Techniques: Button-Fastening Cushion. To finish, bind the cushion edge (see General Techniques: Binding).

PATCHWORK PUMPKINS

These plump pumpkins in four different sizes make wonderful decorations at any time of year. The pumpkins are shown in different fabric combinations from the Harvest collection. Materials and instructions are given for the large pumpkin, so you will need slightly less fabric for the small and medium pumpkins and slightly more for the extra-large.

Finished Sizes
Small: 6in x 5in (15cm x 13cm)
Medium: 6¾in x 6in (17cm x 15cm)
Large: 6¾in x 7½in (17cm x 19cm)
Extra-Large: 11in x 10¾in (28cm x 27cm)

MATERIALS

- Eight print fabrics 4in x 13in (10.2cm x 33cm) of each, for pumpkin body
- One print fabric 7½in x 5in (19cm x 12.7cm), for stalk
- Wooden stick for turning through and stuffing
- Toy stuffing
- Long doll needle
- Embroidery thread

Preparation

1 Before you start, refer to the notes in General Techniques: Making Quilts and Pillows. The pumpkins use the same fabrics as the Pumpkin Harvest Quilt, so refer to **Fig A** there for the fabric swatches if needed.

2 Choose the size of pumpkin you wish to make, copy the relevant pattern pieces from the Patterns section and cut out the shapes. The pumpkin body pattern is given as one half of the design. Draw the half pattern and then flip the pattern to finish drawing the complete shape. Note: The pumpkin sections have a seam allowance added, so the dashed line is the sewing line and the solid outer line is the cutting line. The pumpkin stalks do *not* have a seam allowance added, so the solid line is the sewing line.

3 Use the complete pumpkin pattern to draw eight shapes, each in a different fabric.

Making a Pumpkin

4 To sew a pumpkin body together take the eight sections and arrange them in order. Sew the sections together in pairs, as follows. Take the first two sections and place them right sides together. With a pencil, mark a dot ¾in (2cm) away from the top and bottom points (**Fig A**). Sew a ¼in (6mm) seam down the long side, starting and stopping at these marked points. It's a good idea to backstitch for a few stitches at the start and finish of the seam to secure the stitching. Turn to the right side and press. Repeat this with the other three pairs.

FIG A

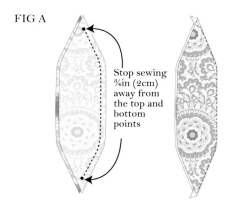

Stop sewing ¾in (2cm) away from the top and bottom points

5 Now sew the pairs together, starting and stopping at the ends of the sewn seams. On the final seam, leave a gap in the straight section for turning through. Turn the pumpkin through to the right side and stuff it well. Hand sew up the gap (**Fig B**).

FIG B

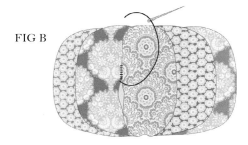

6 To turn the ball into a pumpkin shape, thread the long doll needle with the embroidery thread. Pass the needle through the top of the pumpkin, down and out of the bottom, leaving a long tail at the top of the pumpkin. Make a small stitch sideways and then take the needle back up to the top again. Remove the needle, tie the threads together

and pull really firmly on both of the threads, to create a squashed shape and an indentation at the top and bottom. Use the needle to feed the thread tails into the pumpkin.

7 To make the stalk, take the 7½in x 5in (19cm x 12.7cm) piece of fabric and fold it in half, right sides together. Mark the stalk pattern and sew, using a smaller stitch length of about 1.6. Cut out with a seam allowance and snip notches in the inward curves (**Fig C1**). Turn through to the right side, turn the seam allowance under and press in place (**Fig C2**). Stuff the stalk with the help of a wooden stick. Sew around the opening and pull up the thread to form a gathered neck.

FIG C

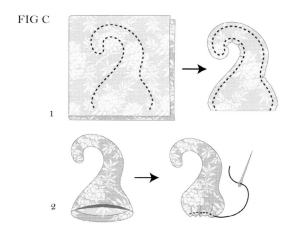

1

2

8 Squeeze the bottom of the stalk against the dent in the top of the pumpkin and create a round shape using pins. Now hand sew the stalk to the pumpkin to finish (**Fig D**).

FIG D

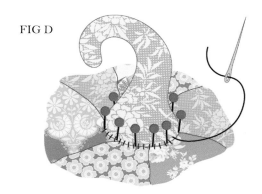

COTTAGE QUILT

This adorable quilt will be such a lovely addition to any home. It is created with a 'cottage' block and a 'tree' block, repeated in different fabric combinations and separated by narrow sashing. It uses fabrics from the Cottage collection.

Finished Size 52in x 77in (132cm x 195.5cm)

FIG A
Fabric swatches
If you can't get hold of one or more of these fabrics,
just replace with fabrics in similar colours

 Fabric 1
Solid
off-white

 Fabric 12
Botanical
sage

 Fabric 2
Botanical
red

 Fabric 13
Sigrid
dove white

 Fabric 3
Sigrid
red

 Fabric 14
Berry Leaf
sage

 Fabric 4
Minnie
red

 Fabric 15
Minerva
dove white

 Fabric 5
Berry Leaf
red

 Fabric 16
Fireworks
sage

 Fabric 6
Minerva
red

 Fabric 17
Berry Leaf
blue

 Fabric 7
Berry Leaf
plum

 Fabric 18
Minnie
blue

 Fabric 8
Botanical
plum

 Fabric 19
Botanical
blue

 Fabric 9
Fireworks
red

 Fabric 20
Minerva
blue

 Fabric 10
Sigrid
plum

 Fabric 21
Sigrid
blue

 Fabric 11
Minnie
plum

MATERIALS

- Fabric 1: 2¼yd (2m) – Solid off white
- Fabric 2: ⅜yd (40cm) – Botanical red
- Fabric 3: ¼yd (25cm) – Sigrid red
- Fabric 4: ¼yd (25cm) – Minnie red
- Fabric 5: ¼yd (25cm) – Berry Leaf red
- Fabric 6: ¼yd (25cm) – Minerva red
- Fabric 7: ¼yd (25cm) – Berry Leaf plum
- Fabric 8: ⅜yd (40cm) – Botanical plum
- Fabric 9: ⅜yd (40cm) – Fireworks red
- Fabric 10: ¼yd (25cm) – Sigrid plum
- Fabric 11: ¼yd (25cm) – Minnie plum
- Fabric 12: ¼yd (25cm) – Botanical sage
- Fabric 13: ¼yd (25cm) – Sigrid dove white
- Fabric 14: ¼yd (25cm) – Berry Leaf sage
- Fabric 15: ¼yd (25cm) – Minerva dove white
- Fabric 16: ¼yd (25cm) – Fireworks sage
- Fabric 17: ⅜yd (40cm) – Berry Leaf blue
- Fabric 18: ⅛yd (15cm) – Minnie blue
- Fabric 19: ¼yd (25cm) – Botanical blue
- Fabric 20: ⅜yd (40cm) – Minerva blue
- Fabric 21: ⅛yd (15cm) – Sigrid blue
- Backing fabric 3⅜yd (3.1m) of standard width
- Wadding (batting) 60in x 85in (152.5cm x 216cm)
- Binding fabric – from multiple fabrics (see instructions)

Preparation and Cutting Out

1 In this quilt there are twenty-four Cottage blocks (in six different colourways) and eighteen Tree blocks (in three different colourways). The blocks are separated by narrow sashing strips. The fabrics used for the quilt are shown in **Fig A** and the quilt layout in **Fig B**.

2 From Fabric 1 for the Cottage blocks cut the following.
- Three 2½in (6.4cm) x width of fabric strips. Sub-cut into forty-eight 2½in (6.4cm) squares.
- Two 4¼in (10.8cm) x width of fabric strips. Sub-cut into forty-eight pieces 1½in x 4¼in (3.8cm x 10.8cm).

FIG B
Quilt layout

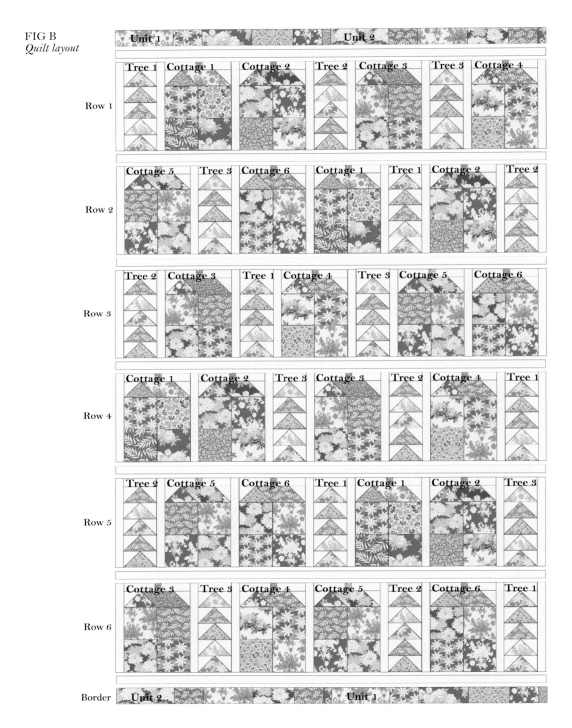

3 From Fabric 1 for the Tree blocks cut the following.
- Seven 2⅞in (7.3cm) x width of fabric strips. Sub-cut into ninety-two 2⅞in (7.3cm) squares.
- Two 1½in (3.8cm) x width of fabric strips. Sub-cut into eighteen pieces 1½in x 4½in (3.8cm x 11.4cm).

4 From Fabric 1 for the sashing cut the following.
- Two 11½in (29.2cm) x width of fabric strips. Sub-cut into forty-eight pieces 11½in x 1½in (29.2cm x 3.8cm) for vertical sashing.
- Nine 1½in (3.8cm) x width of fabric strips. Join end to end, press seams open and sub-cut into seven strips 1½in x 52½in (3.8cm x 133.4cm) for horizontal sashing.

5 From Fabric 2 cut the following.
- Two strips 4½in (11.4cm) x width of fabric. Sub-cut into twelve 4½in (11.4cm) squares and eight pieces 4½in x 2½in (11.4cm x 6.4cm).
- One strip 2½in (6.4cm) x width of fabric. Sub-cut into two pieces 2½in x 4in (6.4cm x 10.2cm) and two pieces 2½in x 1½in (6.4cm x 3.8cm), for border.

6 From Fabric 3 cut one strip 4½in (11.4cm) x width of fabric. Sub-cut into four 4½in (11.4cm) squares, four pieces 4½in x 2½in (11.4cm x 6.4cm) and two pieces 1½in x 2½in (3.8cm x 6.4cm) for border.

7 From Fabric 4 cut the following.
- One strip 4½in (11.4cm) x width of fabric. Sub-cut into eight 4½in (11.4cm) squares.
- One strip 2½in (6.4cm) x width of fabric. Sub-cut into two pieces 2½in x 7½in (6.4cm x 19cm) for border.

8 From Fabric 5 cut the following.
- One strip 4½in (11.4cm) x width of fabric. Sub-cut into eight 4½in (11.4cm) squares.
- One strip 2½in (6.4cm) x width of fabric. Sub-cut into two pieces 2½in x 4in (6.4cm x 10.2cm) for border.

9 From Fabric 6 cut one strip 4½in (11.4cm) x width of fabric. Sub-cut into four 4½in (11.4cm) squares, four pieces 4½in x 2½in (11.4cm x 6.4cm) and two pieces 2½in x 6½in (6.4cm x 16.5cm) for border.

10 From Fabric 7 cut one strip 4½in (11.4cm) x width of fabric. Sub-cut into four 4½in (11.4cm) squares and two pieces 4in x 2½in (10.2cm x 6.4cm) for border.

11 From Fabric 8 cut the following.
- Two strips 4½in (11.4cm) x width of fabric. Sub-cut into sixteen 4½in (11.4cm) squares.
- One strip 2½in (6.4cm) x width of fabric. Sub-cut into two pieces 2½in x 7½in (6.4cm x 19cm) and two pieces 6½in x 2½in (16.5cm x 6.4cm) for border.

12 From Fabric 9 cut the following.
- Two strips 4½in (11.4cm) x width of fabric. Sub-cut into sixteen 4½in (11.4cm) squares.
- One strip 2½in (6.4cm) x width of fabric. Sub-cut into four pieces 2½in x 4½in (6.4cm x 11.4cm) and two pieces 2½in x 4in (6.4cm x 10.2cm) for border.

13 From Fabric 10 cut the following.
- One strip 4½in (11.4cm) x width of fabric. Sub-cut into eight 4½in (11.4cm) squares.
- One strip 2½in (6.4cm) x width of fabric. Sub-cut into four pieces 2½in x 4½in (6.4cm x 11.4cm) and two pieces 2½in x 5½in (6.4cm x 14cm) for border.

14 From Fabric 11 cut the following.
- One strip 4½in (11.4cm) x width of fabric. Sub-cut into eight 4½in (11.4cm) squares.
- One strip 2½in (6.4cm) x width of fabric. Sub-cut into two pieces 2½in x 5½in (6.4cm x 14cm) for border.

15 From the following fabrics cut the stated numbers of 5¼in (13.3cm) squares for flying geese units.
- Fabric 12 cut six squares.

- Fabric 13 cut five squares.
- Fabric 14 cut six squares.
- Fabric 16 cut six squares.

16 From Fabric 15 cut one strip 4½in (11.4cm) x width of fabric. Sub-cut into eight 4½in (11.4cm) squares.

17 From Fabric 17 cut one strip 6½in (16.5cm) x width of fabric. Sub-cut into eight pieces 6½in x 2½in (16.5cm x 6.4cm) and eight pieces 1½in x 1in (3.8cm x 2.5cm).

18 From Fabric 18 cut one strip 2½in (6.4cm) x width of fabric. Sub-cut into four pieces 2½in x 6½in (6.4cm x 16.5cm).

19 From Fabric 19 cut one strip 2½in (6.4cm) x width of fabric. Sub-cut into four pieces 2½in x 6½in (6.4cm x 16.5cm).

20 From Fabric 20 cut one strip 2½in (6.4cm) x width of fabric. Sub-cut into four pieces 2½in x 6½in (6.4cm x 16.5cm).

21 From Fabric 21 cut one strip 2½in (6.4cm) x width of fabric and sub-cut into four pieces 2½in x 6½in (6.4cm x 16.5cm) and sixteen pieces 1½in x 1in (3.8cm x 2.5cm).

22 From the backing fabric cut two pieces 60in (155cm) x width of fabric. Remove selvedges, sew the pieces together along the long side and press the seam open. You will need a piece approximately 60in x 85in (155cm x 216cm).

23 The binding is a scrappy one made up of Fabrics 17, 19 and 20. From Fabrics 17 and 19 cut two strips 2½in x 40in (6.4cm x 101.6cm). From Fabric 20 cut three strips. Place the seven strips in a repeating order. Sew the strips together end to end using straight seams and then press seams open. Press the binding in half along the length, wrong sides together.

Making the Cottage Blocks

24 All of the Cottage blocks are made in the same way, but with six different fabric combinations. **Fig C** shows the units and cut measurements that make up one block. Detailed instructions are given here for making Cottage block 1. Start by piecing the roof unit. **Fig D1** shows the cut pieces and fabrics needed. Follow **Fig D2–D7** carefully. Place a 2½in (6.4cm) square of off-white right sides together with the longest rectangle of Fabric 19, aligning edges. Mark a diagonal line on the light square and sew along this line, as shown. Place the shorter rectangle of Fabric 3 perpendicular to Fabric 19 (right sides together), mark the diagonal and

sew along the line, as shown. Trim off excess fabric leaving a ¼in (6mm) seam allowance and press. Add the remaining 2½in (6.4cm) square to the left-hand end of the pieced unit, creating a triangle and then trim and press as before. The finished roof unit should be 2½in x 8½in (6.4cm x 21.6cm).

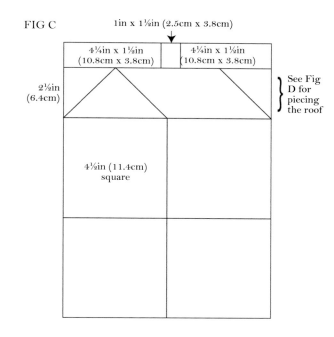

FIG C

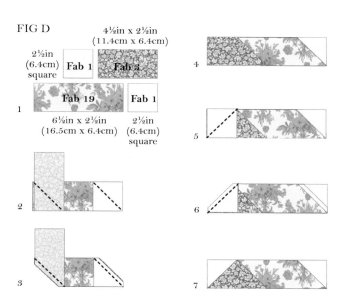

FIG D

25 Piece the Cottage block together following **Fig E**. Check the sewn block is 8½in x 11½in (21.6cm x 29.2cm).

26 Following the fabric combinations shown in **Fig F**, make twenty-four Cottage blocks in total – four each of block 1, block 2, block 3, block 4, block 5 and block 6. Put the blocks into six labelled piles so you can find the correct ones later.

four at once, using one 5¼in (13.3cm) print square and four 2⅞in (7.3cm) off-white squares, following the instructions in General Techniques: Flying Geese – Four at Once. Check each sewn unit is 4½in x 2½in (11.4cm x 6.4cm).

28 Repeat this process to make the remaining flying geese units. You will need the following.
- Twenty-four of flying geese unit 1.
- Twenty-four of flying geese unit 2.
- Twenty-four of flying geese unit 3.
- Twenty of flying geese unit 4 (two will be spare).
-

FIG E

FIG F

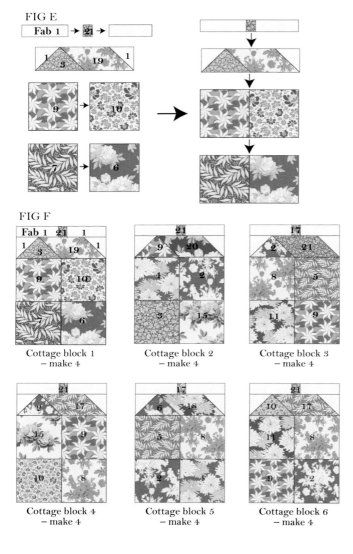

Cottage block 1
– make 4

Cottage block 2
– make 4

Cottage block 3
– make 4

Cottage block 4
– make 4

Cottage block 5
– make 4

Cottage block 6
– make 4

FIG G

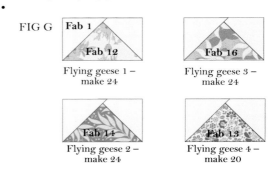

Flying geese 1 –
make 24

Flying geese 3 –
make 24

Flying geese 2 –
make 24

Flying geese 4 –
make 20

29 Now follow **Fig H** to piece the flying geese units together into blocks. Each Tree block needs a 1½in x 4½in (3.8cm x 11.4cm) piece of off-white on the top. Put the blocks into three labelled piles.

FIG H

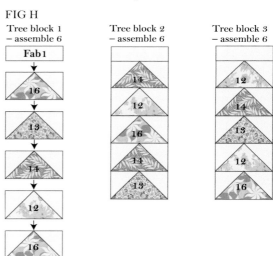

Tree block 1
– assemble 6

Tree block 2
– assemble 6

Tree block 3
– assemble 6

Making the Tree Blocks

27 Each Tree block is made up of five flying geese units with a narrow rectangle on top. The blocks are made in the same way, but with three different combinations of flying geese units. **Fig G** shows the fabric combinations for the individual flying geese units. Make the flying geese units

Making the Borders

30 The quilt has a border at the top and at the bottom. Each is made up of two pieced units – Unit 1 and Unit 2. Unit 1 uses Fabrics 8, 9, 6, 10, 2 and 3. Unit 2 uses Fabrics 4, 7, 8, 11, 5 and 2. The sizes of the fabric pieces are given in **Fig I** (you have already cut these pieces in Cutting Out). For Unit 1 sew the pieces together end to end in the order shown and press seams open or to one side. Make a second unit like this. Repeat the process for Unit 2, following the order shown. Make a second unit like this. For the top border, sew a Unit 2 to the end of a Unit 1. For the bottom border reverse this and sew a Unit 1 to the end of a Unit 2.

FIG I

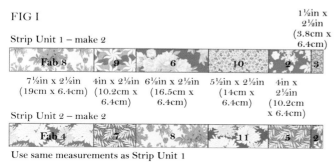

Strip Unit 1 – make 2

Fab 8	9	6	10	2	3
7½in x 2½in (19cm x 6.4cm)	4in x 2½in (10.2cm x 6.4cm)	6½in x 2½in (16.5cm x 6.4cm)	5½in x 2½in (14cm x 6.4cm)	4in x 2½in (10.2cm x 6.4cm)	1½in x 2½in (3.8cm x 6.4cm)

Strip Unit 2 – make 2

Fab 4	7	8	11	5	2

Use same measurements as Strip Unit 1

Assembling the Quilt

31 Take all of your blocks and lay them out in the order shown in **Fig B**. The blocks are labelled to show where each colourway should go. Start by sewing Row 1 together, sewing an off-white sashing strip 1½in x 11½in (3.8cm x 29.2cm) between each block and at the ends of the row. Press seams open or to one side. Repeat this process to sew each row together. Now sew the rows together, sewing a long off-white sashing strip 1½in x 52½in (3.8cm x 133.3cm) between each of the rows and at the top and bottom of the quilt. Press seams open or to one side. To finish the piecing, sew the top border to the quilt and then the bottom border and press.

Quilting and Finishing

32 Make a quilt sandwich of the backing fabric, wadding (batting) and quilt. Quilt as desired. Square up the quilt, trimming excess wadding and backing.

33 Use the prepared binding to bind your quilt – see General Techniques: Binding. Add a label to your lovely quilt to finish.

COTTAGE PILLOWS

*These pretty pillows feature blocks from the Cottage Quilt and use some of the same fabrics, so refer to the fabric swatches in **Fig A** of the quilt. Instructions and materials are given for the long pillow. The short pillow uses the same techniques but different fabrics and fewer blocks.*

Finished Sizes
Long pillow: 38in x 13in (96.5cm x 33cm)
Short pillow: 15in x 13in (38cm x 33cm)

MATERIALS

Long Pillow
- Fabric 1: ⅜yd (40cm) – Solid off-white
- Small pieces of the print fabrics (except Fabric 18) – maximum of 9in (23cm) square
- Wadding (batting) 42in x 17in (106.7cm x 43.2cm)
- Lining fabric 42in x 17in (106.7cm x 43.2cm) (optional)
- Fabric for back of cushion, two pieces 23in x 13½in (58.4cm x 34.3cm)
- Binding fabric – scrappy binding from three fabrics (see instructions)
- Three ¾in (2cm) buttons for pillow back

LONG COTTAGE PILLOW

1 From Fabric 1 cut the following pieces.
- Six pieces 4¼in x 1½in (10.8cm x 3.8cm) for Cottage blocks.
- Six 2½in (6.4cm) squares for Cottage blocks.
- Two pieces 4½in x 1½in (11.4cm x 3.8cm) for Tree blocks.
- Twenty 2½in (6.4cm) squares, for Tree block flying geese (see Step 9).
- Six strips 1½in x 11½in (3.8cm x 29.2cm) for sashing.
- Two strips 1½in x 38½in (3.8cm x 97.8cm) for sashing.

2 Cut 4½in (11.4cm) squares from the print fabrics, cutting one from Fabric 2, 3, 4, 5, 6, 7, 8, 10, 11 and 15. Cut two from Fabric 9.

3 From Fabrics 19, 20 and 21 cut one piece 6½in x 2½in (16.5cm x 6.4cm).

4 From Fabrics 3, 9 and 2 cut one piece 4½in x 2½in (11.4cm x 6.4cm).

5 From Fabric 17 cut one piece 1in x 1½in (2.5cm x 3.8cm). Cut two pieces from Fabric 21.

6 From Fabrics 13, 14 and 12 cut two pieces 4½in x 2½in (11.4cm x 6.4cm), for flying geese (see Step 2). Cut four pieces from Fabric 16.

7 For the binding, from Fabrics 19, 17 and 20 cut two strips each 2½in x 18½in (6.4cm x 47cm). Sew together in a repeating order and prepare as a double-fold binding.

8 To make the long pillow, follow the Cottage Quilt instructions to make the blocks, making one Block 1, one Block 2 and one Block 3. **Fig A** here shows the blocks and fabrics used.

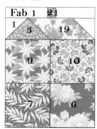
Cottage block 1

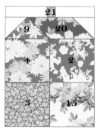
Cottage block 2

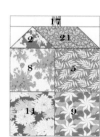
Cottage block 3

FIG A

9 Make two of Tree block 1, as in **Fig B** here. If you are only making the pillow and not the quilt too, then make *individual* flying geese units, with one print rectangle 2½in x 4½in (6.4cm x 11.4cm) and two off-white 2½in (6.4cm) squares (for instructions see General Techniques: Flying Geese – Single Unit).

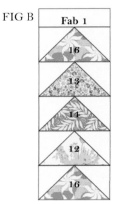

FIG B

Tree block 1 – make 2

10 Place the blocks in the order shown in **Fig C** here, with short sashing strips between the blocks and at both ends. Sew together and press. Add the long sashing strips to the top and bottom of the patchwork and press.

FIG C

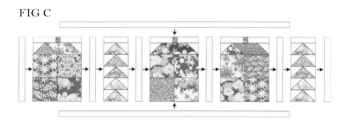

11 Make a quilt sandwich of the patchwork, wadding (batting) and the lining fabric (if using). Quilt as desired.

12 The pillow is assembled with an overlapped back, with buttons to secure. Use the two pieces of fabric for the cushion back and follow the instructions in See General Techniques: Button-Fastening Cushion. To finish, use the prepared binding to bind the cushion edge (see General Techniques: Binding).

SHORT COTTAGE PILLOW

This pillow uses just one Cottage block 4 and one Tree block 1 from the Cottage Quilt, with 1½in (3.8cm) sashing strips. Follow **Fig D** here for the blocks and **Fig E** here for the pillow assembly. Once pieced, the patchwork is 15½in x 13½in (39.4cm x 34.3cm). Make a quilt sandwich and quilt as desired. Make up the cushion in the same way as the Long Pillow, using fabric pieces suitable for the size of this pillow. For the binding, from fabrics 19, 17 and 20 cut one strip 2½in x 21in (6.4cm x 53.3cm).

FIG D

Cottage block 4   Tree block 1

FIG E

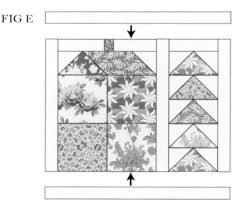

PATCHWORK SANTA

This endearing Santa in his festive red and white is sure to be a favourite decoration for Christmas time, making a welcome appearance year after year.

Finished Size 12in x 20½in (30.5cm x 52cm)

MATERIALS
- Fabric 1: one fat quarter – Solid off-white
- Fabric 2: one fat quarter – Doll fabric
- Fabric 3: one fat quarter – Minnie red
- Fabric 4: one fat quarter – Berry Leaf red
- Fabric 5: one fat quarter – Botanical plum
- Fabric 6: ½yd (50cm) – Sigrid plum
- Wadding (batting) 40in x 20in (100cm x 50cm)
- Paper piece glue (optional)
- Wooden stick for turning and stuffing
- Disappearing marker pen

Preparation

1 Before you start, refer to the notes in General Techniques: Making Softies. Copy all pattern pieces from the Patterns section onto thick paper and cut out the shapes. The fabrics used are shown in **Fig A**.

Making Santa

2 Body: Cut and sew together a strip of doll body fabric 21¼in x 10in (54cm x 25.5cm) and a 21¼in x 7½in (54cm x 19cm) strip of Fabric 6 and press open. Fold the pieced strip in half, right sides together. Draw the body pattern, lining up the dashed line across the body with the seam in the fabrics. Sew as shown in **Fig B**. Note that the in-turning corners and the area marked as an opening on the pattern should be left open. Cut out the body with a seam allowance all round. Fold each corner so that the seams are over and under each other, as in **Fig C**, to create depth to the body. Pin, if needed. Sew across the corners as in **Fig D**. Turn through to the right side and press.

FIG A
Fabric swatches
If you can't get hold of one or more of these fabrics, just replace with fabrics in similar colours

 Fabric 1
Solid
off-white

 Fabric 5
Botanical
plum

 Fabric 2
Doll fabric

 Fabric 6
Sigrid
plum

 Fabric 3
Minnie
red

 Fabric 4
Berry Leaf
red

FIG B
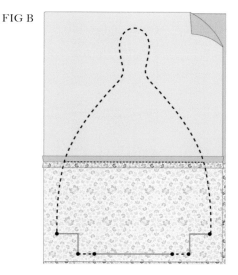

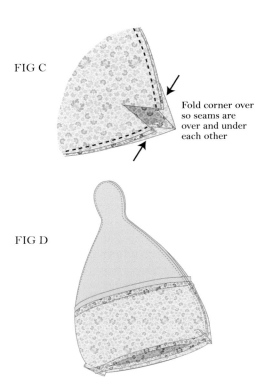

FIG C

Fold corner over
so seams are
over and under
each other

FIG D

4 Arms: Fold the remainder of the doll body fabric double and draw two arms using the arm pattern. Mark the openings and sew around the arms. Cut out with a seam allowance, turn through to the right side and press. Stuff the arms using the stick and tack (baste) the openings shut. Sew the arms onto the body just below the neck (**Fig F**).

5 Jacket: The jacket has a pieced front and a pieced back. **Fig G** shows the pieces to cut for the front, and **Fig H** for the back. For the front you will also need to make four Flying Geese blocks and one appliqué star block.

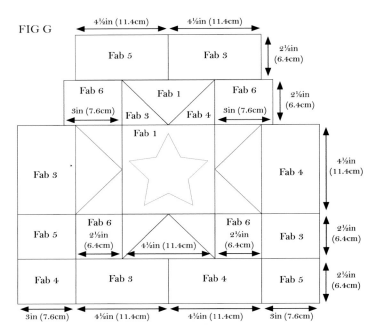

FIG G

3 Legs: Cut a 10in x 4½in (25.4cm x 11.4cm) strip of Fabric 4, a 10in x 2½in (25.5cm x 6.4cm) strip of Fabric 3 and a 10in x 4in (25.4cm x 10.2cm) strip of Fabric 6. Sew them together with a ¼in (6mm) seam and press open. Fold the pieced fabric in half, right sides together, as in **Fig E**. Draw the leg pattern twice, lining up the dashed lines on the leg pattern with the seams in the fabrics. Sew, leaving the tops open. Cut out the legs with a seam allowance, turn through with a wooden stick and press. Stuff the legs. Place them about 2⅜in (7cm) apart in the opening of the body. Sew the opening shut, attaching the legs at the same time (**Fig F**).

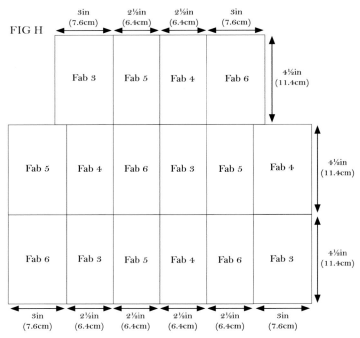

FIG H

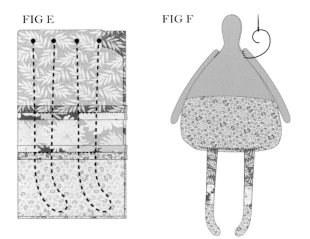

FIG E   FIG F

6 Make a Flying Geese block with one 4½in x 2½in (11.4cm x 6.4cm) rectangle of Fabric 1, one 2½in (6.4cm) square of Fabric 3 and one of Fabric 4. Follow the instructions in General Techniques: Flying Geese – Single Unit. Check the block is 4½in x 2½in (11.4cm x 6.4cm). Repeat to make four Flying Geese blocks in total.

7 Make the appliqué star block with paper-pieced appliqué. Cut a 4½in (11.4cm) square of Fabric 1 and Fabric 6. Draw the star pattern on the back of the print fabric. Cut out the fabric star with a ¼in (6mm) seam allowance (**Fig I**). Place the paper star on the wrong side of the fabric and use a little glue to fix. Snip into the seam allowance where shown on the diagram. Spread glue along the edge of the paper shape and fold the seam allowance over the shape (glue the star points in place first), working around the star. Stitch the star onto the centre of the off-white square with tiny stitches and matching thread. Try not to stitch through the paper. Remove the paper by cutting through the background fabric *only* at the back of the block and coaxing out the paper. Use tweezers to get small pieces out. Press the work.

FIG I

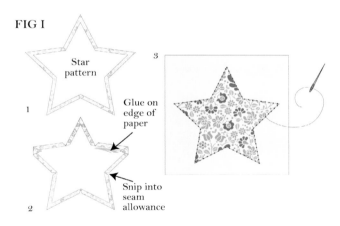

8 Take the star block, the Flying Geese blocks and the other pieces cut for the jacket front and lay them out as in **Fig J**. Using ¼in (6mm) seams, sew the pieces together in rows and press. Sew the rows together and press. Repeat to piece the back of the jacket.

FIG J

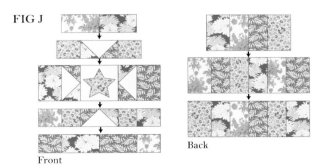

Front

Back

9 Place the jacket front patchwork right side up on a piece of wadding (batting) (**Fig K**). Draw the front pattern using a disappearing pen. Sew a zigzag seam outside the drawn line, and then cut out the jacket shape with seam allowance (**Fig L**). Repeat for the jacket back.

FIG K

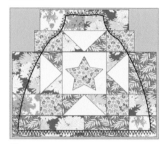 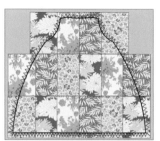

Front   Back

FIG L

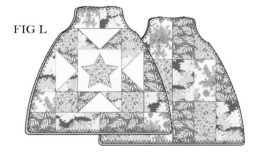

10 To make the sleeves, cut a 9in x 5½in (23cm x 14cm) piece of Fabric 3 and a 9in x 3in (23cm x 7.6cm) piece of Fabric 6. Sew the fabrics together along the long side and press open. Mark the sleeve pattern twice on the wrong side of the pieced fabric, lining up the dashed line on the pattern with the join in the fabric. Cut out the two fabric sleeves, remembering the extra seam allowance (ES) along the edge of the sleeve opening, as marked on the pattern. Mark and cut out two sleeves in wadding (batting), *without* a seam allowance along the edge of the sleeve opening. Place the wadding sleeves on the wrong side of the fabric sleeves. Fold the fabric in along the edge of the sleeve opening, twice, over the wadding. Sew along the edge to keep the fabric in place. Sew a zigzag stitch around the rest of the sleeve to keep the fabric and wadding together (**Fig M**).

FIG M

11 Place the jacket front and back right sides together and sew together along the shoulders. Fold in the neckline seam allowance and tack (baste) to the inside of the jacket (**Fig N**). Open out the jacket and pin the sleeves in place, right sides together and matching the curve of the top of the sleeve with the curve of the jacket. Sew the sleeves to the jacket (**Fig O**). Fold the jacket right sides together and sew along the underside of the sleeves and the sides of the jacket (**Fig P**). Turn the jacket through to the right side and press.

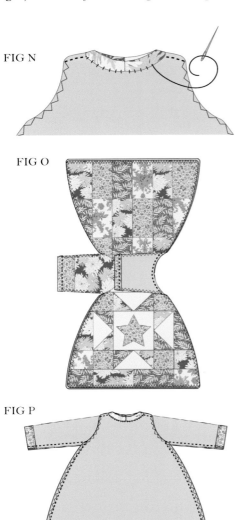

FIG N

FIG O

FIG P

12 For the scalloped edge on the jacket, cut a Fabric 6 strip 26in x 4½in (66cm x 11.4cm). Fold it in half right sides together, draw the full scalloped pattern and sew along the 'bows' (**Fig Q**). Cut out with a seam allowance. Cut notches between every 'bow' where the seams turn in. Turn through to the right side using the wooden stick and press.

Attach the scalloped edge along the bottom edge of the jacket as shown in **Fig R**, so that the extra seam allowance extends beyond the edge of the jacket. The seam should be in alignment with the dotted line in the pattern. Doing it this way means you can fold in the extra seam allowance and attach it to the inside of the jacket, as shown. Iron the scalloped edge down. Fold in the edge and tack (baste) it to the inside of the jacket. Put the jacket onto Santa now.

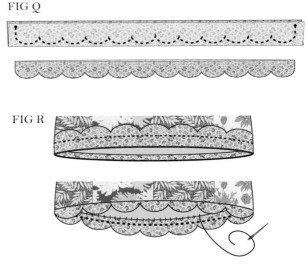

FIG Q

FIG R

13 Hat: Cut two 6½in x 2½in (16.5cm x 6.4cm) strips from Fabric 5, Fabric 3, Fabric 6 and Fabric 4. Sew the eight strips of fabric together in the order shown in **Fig S** and press seams open. Cut a piece of wadding (batting) the same size as the pieced unit, placing it on the back of the pieced section. Fold the layered work in half, with the pieced section right sides together, as in **Fig T**. Use the hat pattern to draw the shape and then sew. Cut out with a seam allowance. Turn through to the right side with a wooden stick. Fold up the extra seam allowance around the opening to the wrong side, tack (baste) in place and press.

FIG S

Fabric 5
Fabric 3
Fabric 6
Fabric 4

Wadding (batting)

14 Beard and Face: Fold an 8in x 5in (20.3cm x 12.7cm) piece of off-white fabric in half, right sides together, and lay a 4in x 5in (10.2cm x 12.7cm) piece of wadding (batting) beneath. Using the beard pattern, draw the shape and sew all the way around (**Fig U**). Cut out the beard and make a slit through just one of the fabric layers. Turn right side out through the slit and press the beard. Sew up the slit with a few stitches. The beard looks lovely if you hand quilt it (see photo). Pin the beard and hat onto Santa.

FIG U

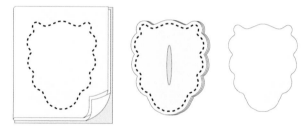

15 To make the face, see General Techniques: Faces. Use black hobby paint, a little lipstick or rouge and a dry brush. Place two small metal-headed pins in the head to see where the eyes should be in relation to the hat and beard. Remove the hat and beard to avoid getting paint on them. Remove the eye pins. Dip the pin in black paint, stamp over the pin holes and then allow to dry. Brush on some rouge with a dry brush. Pin the beard and hat on again, tack (baste) into place and then remove pins. Your sweet Santa is now complete.

PATCHWORK STOCKING

Imagine this over-sized stocking filled with gifts! What more could you want waiting for you on Christmas morning? The stocking is shown as a red and a blue version, with the red one described here.

Finished Size 14in x 22¼in (35.5cm x 56.5cm)

MATERIALS

Red Stocking
- Fabric 1: ¾yd (75cm) – Solid off-white
- Fabric 2: one fat quarter – Minerva red
- Fabric 3: one fat quarter – Sigrid plum
- Fabric 4: one fat quarter – Botanical blue
- Fabric 5: one fat quarter – Berry Leaf red
- Fabric 6: one fat quarter – Minerva dove white
- Wadding (batting) 25in x 35in (63.5cm x 89cm)
- Paper piece glue (optional)

FIG A
Fabric swatches for the red stocking
If you can't get hold of one or more of these fabrics, just replace with fabrics in similar colours

 Fabric 1
Solid
off-white

 Fabric 5
Berry Leaf
red

 Fabric 2
Minerva
red

 Fabric 6
Minerva dove
white

 Fabric 3
Sigrid
plum

 Fabric 4
Botanical
blue

Preparation

1 Before you start, refer to the notes in General Techniques: Making Quilts and Pillows. Copy all pattern pieces from the Patterns section onto thick paper and cut out the shapes. Tape the stocking parts together on the dashed lines. Use the star pattern from the Patchwork Santa project.

Making the Patchwork

2 Six fabrics are used for the stocking (**Fig A**). It is lined with Fabric 1. The patchwork for the front of the stocking is different to the back patchwork. Follow **Fig B** for the pieces to cut for the front and **Fig C** for the back. For the front, you will also need to make four Flying Geese blocks and one appliqué star block.

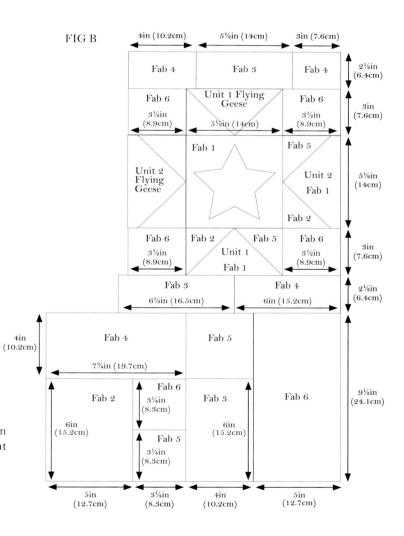

FIG B

FIG C

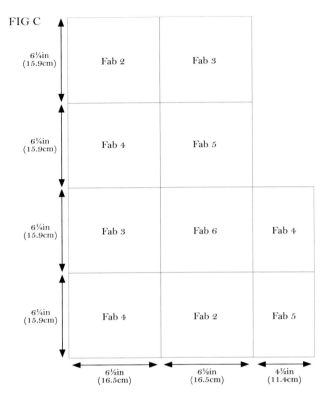

5 Make the appliqué star block with paper-pieced appliqué. Cut a 5½in (14cm) square of Fabric 1 and of Fabric 3. Use the stocking star pattern to draw the shape on the back of the print fabric. Follow the appliqué instructions for Step 7 of the Patchwork Santa project.

6 Take the star block, the Flying Geese blocks and the other pieces you cut for the stocking front and lay them out as in **Fig F**. Sew the pieces together and press seams open. Now sew the rows together and press.

7 Take the pieces you cut for the stocking back and sew them together with ¼in (6mm) seams as in **Fig G** and press.

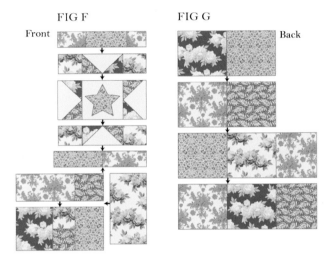

FIG F — Front

FIG G — Back

3 There are two sizes of Flying Geese used on the front of the stocking – two units are 5½in x 3in (14cm x 7.6cm) (Unit 1) and two units are 5½in x 3½in (14cm x 8.9cm) (Unit 2). To make a Unit 1 Flying Geese block use a 5½in x 3in (14cm x 7.6cm) rectangle of Fabric 1, one 3in (7.6cm) square of Fabric 2 and one square of Fabric 5. Follow **Fig D** here and the instructions in General Techniques: Flying Geese – Single Unit. Check the block is 5½in x 3in (14cm x 7.6cm). Repeat to make a second Unit 1 Flying Geese block.

Stocking Assembly

8 Cut a piece of Fabric 1 about 17in x 25in (43.2cm x 63.5cm) and one the same size in wadding (batting). Place them under the patchwork for the front of the stocking (**Fig H**). Use the full stocking pattern to mark the shape. Sew on the line, leaving the top open. Cut out with a *scant* ¼in (6mm) seam allowance (**Fig I**). Quilt as desired.

9 Do the same with the patchwork for the back of the stocking. Note that this time the pattern has to be facing the *opposite* way (**Fig J**). Cut out with a *scant* seam allowance all round (**Fig K**). Quilt as desired.

FIG D — Unit 1 Flying Geese – make 2

4 A Unit 2 Flying Geese block is ½in (1.3cm) taller than a Unit 1 but is made in the same way. Follow **Fig E**, cutting a 5½in x 3½in (14cm x 8.9cm) rectangle of Fabric 1, one 3in (7.6cm) square of Fabric 2 and one square of Fabric 5.

FIG E — Unit 2 Flying Geese – make 2

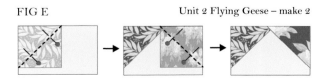

FIG H

FIG I

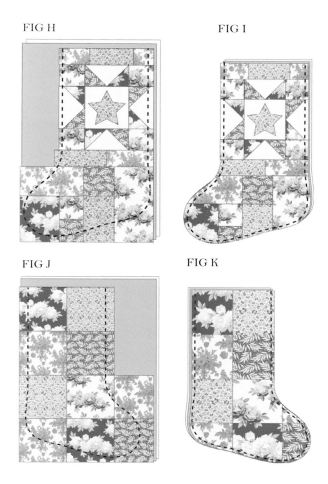

FIG J

FIG K

binding instructions in General Techniques: Binding. Turn the binding over to the inside of the stocking, slipstitch in place all round and then press.

FIG N

12 To make a loop to hang the stocking, cut a Fabric 6 strip 1¾in x 7½in (4.5cm x 19cm). Fold over and press a ¼in (6mm) seam allowance along the two short sides and then down each long side. Fold the strip in half along the length, wrong sides together, and sew together. Fold the strip in half and sew the loop firmly to the inside of the stocking, at the back to finish.

10 Place front and back of the stocking right sides together and sew together all round the edge with a generous ¼in (6mm) seam allowance, leaving the top open (**Fig L**). Zigzag stitch around the seam allowance (**Fig M**). Turn through to the right side and finger-press the seam, making sure it is properly turned out.

FIG L

Place the two quilt sandwiches right sides together and sew together

FIG M

Zigzag stitch the seam allowance

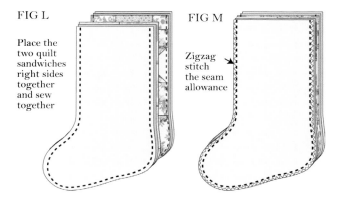

11 Bind the top of the stocking using a Fabric 2 strip 2¼in (6cm) x about 25in (63.5cm). Press the strip in half along the length, wrong sides together. Follow **Fig N** and the

MATERIALS

Tilda fabrics and other materials are used predominantly for the projects in this book. The print fabrics come from the following Tilda collections: 'Cabbage Rose' Autumn/Winter 2016, 'Bumblebee' Spring 2017, 'Circus' Summer 2017, 'Harvest' Autumn 2017 and 'Cottage' Winter 2017. If you are not able to get hold of a fabric you can easily replace it with another fabric of similar colour (see Choosing Fabrics, below). Many of the smaller projects only use small quantities of fabrics and you can put your off-cuts to good use. Plain-dyed and solid off-white fabric is used in most of the patchwork projects as a contrast to the print fabrics, and on the fox face. Tilda doll fabric is used for Santa's skin.

Choosing Fabrics

For each of the projects a list of the fabrics used has been given but of course you can use *any* fabrics from *any* of the Tilda collections, which gives you an excitingly wide choice of lovely fabrics to use. This also means that you can create your own individual look for a project.

The easiest way to change the fabrics used is to create a 'swatch sheet': make a list of the fabric numbers, Fabric 1, Fabric 2, Fabric 3, and so on, with the name and colour of the fabric you want to use next to it. You could also cut small swatches of the fabrics you have chosen and stick these beside the information. In this way, you can customize a project just for you. See the Tilda fabric collections and related products at www.tildasworld.com

Backing Fabric

The quilts give the yardage needed for backing fabric. These amounts allow 4in (10.2cm) extra all round, to allow for the quilt to be long-arm quilted. If you are quilting the project yourself then 2in (5cm) extra all round will be sufficient. The yardage given is based on the normal 42in–44in (107cm–112cm) wide fabric. If you use a wider fabric then the amount needed will need to be re-calculated. You can also sew quilting fabrics together to make a piece big enough for a backing.

Wadding (batting)

The wadding used is your choice and depends on the effect you want to achieve. For a normal flat and firm result, cotton wadding is recommended, especially for the quilts and pillows. If you like a puffy look then a wadding with a higher loft can be used. For quilts, cut the wadding the same size as the backing, allowing extra for quilting.

General Materials and Tools

The project instructions give the fabrics that are needed but you will also need some general materials and tools, including the following.
- Piecing and quilting threads.
- Rotary cutter and mat.
- Quilter's ruler – a 6½in x 24in rectangular ruler and a 12in square ruler are the most useful.
- Sharp fabric scissors.
- Marking tools, such as a water-soluble pen or chalk liner.
- Thick paper or template plastic to make templates.

GENERAL TECHNIQUES

This section describes the general techniques you will need for the projects.
Techniques that are specific to a project are given within the project instructions.

Using the Patterns

All of the patterns for the book are given full size in the Patterns section at the end of the book. To prepare a pattern, trace or photocopy it onto thick paper (including all marks) and cut out the shape. Label the pattern. If a pattern is made up of two or more parts, then use adhesive tape to fix them together along the dashed lines. There are notes at the start of the Patterns section giving further guidance.

Making Softies

Follow these general guidelines when making the soft projects in the book.
- Read all of a project's instructions through before you start.
- The paper patterns for each softie are in the Patterns section, so follow instructions there.
- A piece of fabric may be used for several pattern pieces, so position and cut pieces economically.
- Use a shorter stitch length of about 1.5 for seams that will be stuffed later.
- Where a gap needs to be left, backstitch at both ends to secure the sewing line.
- To get a good shape, cut snips in the seam allowance where seams curve tightly inwards.
- Stuff well, using a wooden stick to make sure you fill small areas such as arms and ears.
- Sew up gaps with matching thread and small slipstitches.

Faces

To make the eyes, we suggest using black hobby paint. You can create eyes by marking their positions first with a pin. For big eyes ¼in (6mm–7mm) diameter, as used in the fox and other patchwork animals, use a large ball-headed pin. To mark where the eyes will be, wiggle the pin back and forth until you have a visible hole. Dip the head of the pin in paint and then stamp eyes on the project. For small eyes ¹⁄₁₆in (1mm–1.5mm) diameter, as used on Santa, use a small metal-headed pin. You could also find something else to use as a stamp, or draw circles and paint on eyes with a thin brush. Once the eyes are in place, you can mark rosy cheeks with a dry brush and a little rouge or lipstick.

Safety

A manufactured toy is tested extensively before it can be put on sale, but when you sew one yourself you must ensure that it is safe. So please bear in mind the following points, especially when sewing for children.
- Don't let children use toys if small parts or buttons have been used in them.
- Be aware that children can be allergic to some materials, so choose with care.
- Make toys strong and resistant to wear and tear by double sewing seams and fastening legs and arms and other loose parts in place securely with strong embroidery thread.
- Take great care not to leave pins or needles in toys.

Washing

Stuffed toys, such as Santa and the Fox are not suitable for washing as the stuffing can move about or become uneven. To clean a toy, wipe it with a damp cloth, but don't soak it. If Tilda rouge has been used this is water-soluble and can easily be re-applied. You can wash toy clothes carefully, either by hand or on a machine delicate wash of 30 degrees. Quilts and pillow covers can be machine washed on a 40-degree programme. Dry naturally where possible.

Making Quilts and Pillows

Follow these general guidelines when making the quilt and pillows in the book.
- Read all the instructions through before you start.
- Fabric quantities are based on a usable width of 42in (107cm).
- Measurements are in imperial inches with metric conversions in brackets. Use only *one* system throughout (preferably imperial as the projects were made using this system).
- Press fabrics before cutting.
- Use ¼in (6mm) seams unless otherwise instructed.
- Press seams open or to one side, as preferred, or according to the project instructions.

Half-Square Triangles – Two at Once

This is the normal way of making half-square triangles, which creates two identical units.

1 Take two different fabric squares (the size given in the project instructions). Pencil mark the diagonal line on the wrong side of one of the squares (**Fig A**).

2 Pin the two squares right sides together, with all outer edges aligned. Sew ¼in (6mm) away from each side of the marked line.

3 Press and then cut the units apart on the marked line.

4 Open out each unit and press the seam (open or to one side as preferred). Check each unit is the size required.

FIG A
Half-square Triangles – two at once

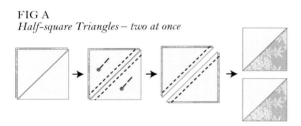

Half-Square Triangles – Four at Once

This method of making half-square triangles is useful as it makes four at the same time.

1 Take two different fabric squares (the size given in the project instructions) and pin them right sides together, matching all edges exactly. Sew around all four sides of the square ¼in (6mm) away from the edge (**Fig B**).

2 Cut the sewn squares into quarters along the diagonals, so you have four triangles. Open out each triangle, press the seam open and trim off the excess little triangles ('dog ears'). Check each unit is the size required.

FIG B
Half-square Triangles – four at once

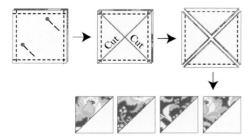

Flying Geese – Single Unit

This method makes one unit at a time and needs one rectangle and two squares. For the flying geese units in the Birds and Sunflowers Quilt the small squares are two different fabrics.

1 On the wrong side of the two small squares, draw or crease a diagonal line. Place the small squares right side down on the rectangle (right side up), aligning the corners as in **Fig C**. Pin together if needed. Sew along the line (or a fraction outside of the line). Trim excess fabric at the back ¼in (6mm) away from the stitching line and press.

2 Sew the second square to the rectangle in the same way in the opposite corner. Once sewn and pressed, this square will overlap the one already sewn in place. This will form the ¼in (6mm) seam allowance.

FIG C
Flying Geese – single unit

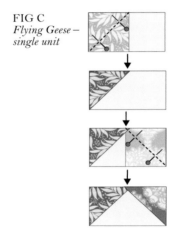

Flying Geese – Four at Once

This method is useful if you have lots and lots of blocks to make as it creates four at the same time.

1 Follow the sequence in **Fig D**. Select one large square and four small squares. Place two small squares right sides together with a large square, aligning them in the corners. Draw a line from corner to corner, as shown. Pin the pieces together and then sew ¼in (6mm) away from the line on both sides (1). Cut apart along the marked line (2) and press the triangles outwards (3).

2 Place one small square right sides together with one of the sewn units. Draw a line as before and sew ¼in (6mm) away from the line on both sides (4). Cut the units apart along the line and press the units (5). Repeat with the last small square and the other sewn unit. You should now have four identical units (6). Check each unit is the size required.

FIG D
Flying Geese – four at once

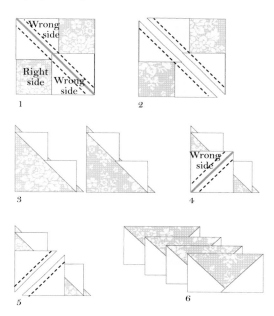

Appliqué

Some of the projects feature appliqué and most of them use paper piece appliqué, where the seam allowance is turned over a paper shape. You can buy a special glue stick for appliqué.

If you prefer, you could use fusible web appliqué, using a fusible web such as Bondaweb (Vliesofix) or Steam-A-Seam. If using fusible web, you will not need a seam allowance around the shapes. Once fused, the shapes will need to be sewn around the edge to secure them, either by machine or with hand stitching.

Quilt Sandwich

If you are quilting the quilt yourself you will need to make a quilt sandwich. Press the quilt top and the backing and smooth wrinkles out of the wadding (batting). Place the backing fabric right side down, place the wadding on top and then the quilt, right side up. Secure the layers of this sandwich. This can be done in various ways, as follows.

• Use large stitches to tack (baste) a grid through the layers in both directions, with lines about 4in (10.2cm) apart.
• Use pins or safety pins to fix the layers together.
• Use fabric glue, sprayed onto the wadding to fix layers.

When the layers of the quilt are secured you can quilt as desired. If you are sending the quilt off to be commercially long-arm quilted you won't need to make a sandwich, as this is done when the quilt is mounted on the machine.

Quilting

There are so many ways to quilt a project. For the quilts in this book you could simply machine or hand stitch 'in the ditch' (that is, in the seams) of each block. Another easy method is to follow the shapes of the block, quilting about ¼in (6mm) away from the seams. If you prefer not to quilt yourself then you could send the quilt top to a long-arm quilter, who will do all the work for you.

Binding

The binding used for the projects in the book is a double-fold binding, using strips cut 2½in (6.4cm) wide x width of fabric. You can sew the binding strips together using straight seams, or diagonal (45-degree) seams if you prefer.

1 When all of the binding strips have been joined together, press in half all along the length, wrong sides together.

2 Follow **Fig E**. Sew the binding to the quilt by pinning the raw edge of the folded binding against the raw edge of the quilt front. Don't start at a corner. Using a ¼in (6mm) seam, sew the binding in place, starting at least 6in (15.2cm) away from the end of the binding. Sew to within a ¼in (6mm) of a corner and stop. Take the quilt off the machine and fold the binding upwards, creating a 45-degree angle. Hold this in place, fold the binding back down and pin it in place. Begin sewing the ¼in (6mm) seam again from the top of the folded binding to within ¼in (6mm) of the next corner and then repeat the folding process. Do this on all corners. Leave about 6in (15.2cm) of unsewn binding at the end.

3 To join the two ends of the binding, open up the beginning and end of the binding tails, lay them flat and fold the ends back so the two ends touch. Mark these folds by creasing – this is where your seam needs to be. Open out the binding and sew the pieces together at these creases with a straight seam. Trim excess fabric and press the seam. Re-fold the binding and finish stitching to the front of the quilt.

4 With the quilt right side up, use a medium-hot iron to press the binding outwards all round. Now begin to turn the binding over to the back of the quilt, pinning it in place. Use matching sewing thread and tiny stitches to slipstitch the binding in place all round, creating neat mitres at each corner. Press the binding and your lovely quilt is finished.

Plain Cushion Cover

The most commonly made cushion cover doesn't usually have any fastenings but just a hemmed opening on the back of the cover, which overlaps at the centre (**Fig F**).

1 Start by calculating the size of the two backing pieces needed, as follows. Measure the width of the cushion or pillow, divide this number in half and then add 4in (10cm). So, for a 20in (50cm) wide pillow, this would be 20in ÷ 2 = 10in (25cm) + 4in (10cm) = 14in (35cm). The height of the pieces will be the same as the front of the cushion.

2 On both pieces of fabric along the short sides, create a hem by turning the edge over by ½in (1.3cm), twice. Sew with matching thread and press.

3 Place the patchwork front right side up. Pin one backing piece on top, right side down and with the hem towards the centre. Pin the second backing piece on top, right side down and with the hem towards the centre. Make sure the outer edges of all three pieces are aligned.

4 To assemble the cover *without* a binding, sew the layers together around the outside, using a ¼in–⅜in (6mm–10mm) seam. Remove pins and press. Turn through to the right side and press.

5 To assemble the cover *with* a binding, pin or tack (baste) the layers together but this time with right sides out, and then bind as normal. As you sew the binding in place it will fix the other layers together.

FIG E
Binding process

Stop ¼in (6mm)
from the end

1

Fold up to create
45-degree angle

2

Fold down and
stitch from the
edge to a ¼in
(6mm) from the
next corner

3

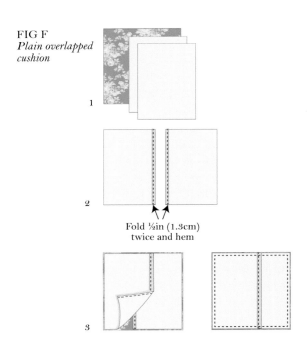

FIG F
*Plain overlapped
cushion*

1

2

Fold ½in (1.3cm)
twice and hem

3

Button-Fastening Cushion

This type of cushion cover is made in the same way as the Plain Cushion Cover but has buttons to fasten the back opening. Most of the pillows in this book were made this way. The buttons can be added with sewn buttonholes or by using snap fasteners behind the buttons (**Fig G**). The cover can also be edged with binding if desired.

1 Start by calculating the size of the two backing pieces needed – see Step 1, Plain Cushion Cover. You could allow less for the overlap if you prefer, as the opening will be fastened by the buttons.

2 On both pieces of fabric along the short sides, create a hem by turning the edge over by 1in (2.5cm), twice. Sew with matching thread. Note: The hem needs to be wide to allow room for buttons. If you are using larger buttons then allow for a wider hem.

3 Decide on which side you want to place your buttons (the diagram shows the left-hand side). With right side up, mark the button positions along the centre of the hem, spacing them equally, and then sew them in place.

4 Measure your button diameter to judge the length of the buttonhole needed. Place the right-hand piece of hemmed fabric next to the left-hand piece and mark with a pencil where the centre of each buttonhole should be. Mark the length of each buttonhole and then create them on your sewing machine or with a tight hand blanket stitch.

FIG G
Button-fastening cushion

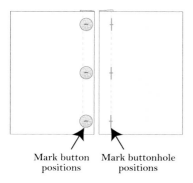 

Mark button   Mark buttonhole
positions   positions

Sew buttonholes

If you want to avoid sewing buttonholes but still want buttons, then sew buttons in place as described above, but add a popper fastener to the back of each button. Sew the other half of the popper in place of the buttonholes.

PATTERNS

- You can download printable versions of the patterns from: www.davidandcharles.com.
- All of the patterns are given at full size.
- Some patterns are shown in a different colour to distinguish them from other patterns.
- The outer solid line on a pattern is the sewing line, unless otherwise stated.
- Dashed black lines show openings.
- Dashed blue lines show where parts of a pattern have to be joined (e.g., by A and B points), which need to be matched.
- Thin dashed lines show a division between two fabrics.
- Short lines on the edges of a pattern show where fabric pieces need to be aligned.
- 'ES' indicates an extra seam allowance, where some projects require a wider allowance. Sew the seam to the end of the extra allowance. Fold under at the inner dotted line (if you are not joining to another piece).
- Some patterns show half of the design, so you will need to mark the pattern and then flip (reverse) it at the dashed line to complete the shape.
- Generally, cut out the shapes after sewing, cutting about ¼in (6mm) outside of the sewn line (cutting by eye is fine).
- For some projects, you will need to add seam allowances to individual pieces – see advice with specific patterns.

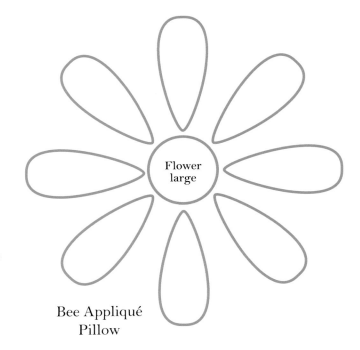

Flower large

Bee Appliqué Pillow

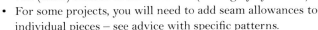

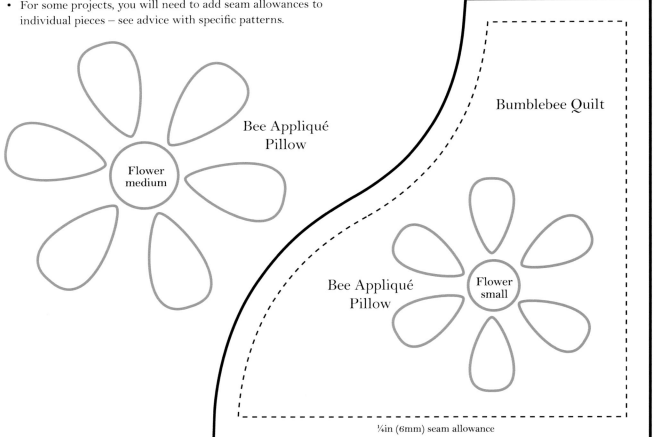

Bee Appliqué Pillow

Flower medium

Bumblebee Quilt

Bee Appliqué Pillow

Flower small

¼in (6mm) seam allowance

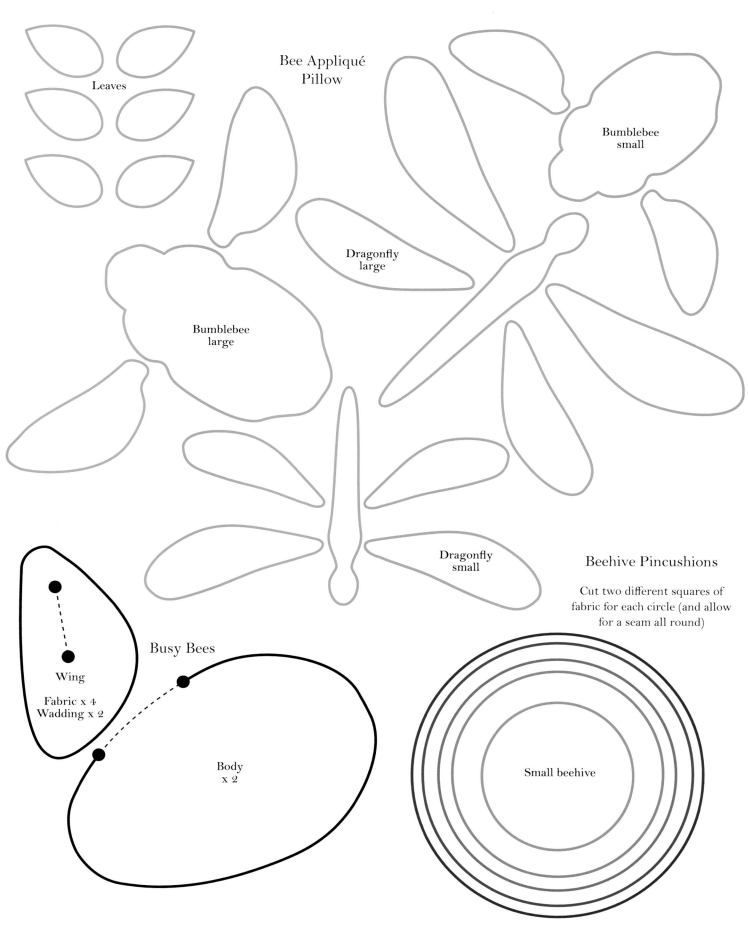

Leaves

Bee Appliqué
Pillow

Bumblebee
small

Dragonfly
large

Bumblebee
large

Dragonfly
small

Beehive Pincushions

Cut two different squares of
fabric for each circle (and allow
for a seam all round)

Busy Bees

Wing

Fabric x 4
Wadding x 2

Body
x 2

Small beehive

119

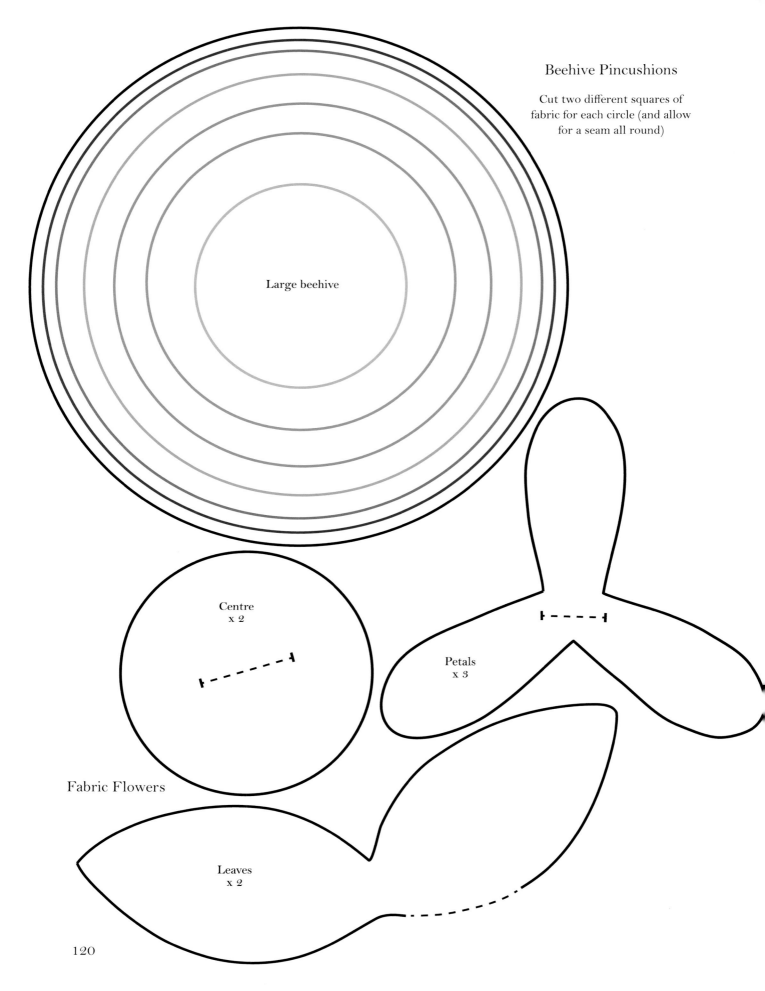

Beehive Pincushions

Cut two different squares of
fabric for each circle (and allow
for a seam all round)

Large beehive

Centre
x 2

Petals
x 3

Fabric Flowers

Leaves
x 2

Tree Pillow

Join the four parts of the
pattern as shown in the
diagram to make one vertical
half of the design. Draw the
half pattern onto one half of
a 26in x 22in (66cm x 56cm)
piece of paper. Flip the pattern
over to draw the other half

Part 1

Part 1

Part 2

Part 4

Part 3

Tree Pillow
Part 2

D

Tree Pillow
Part 3

F

Tree Pillow

Part 4

C

E

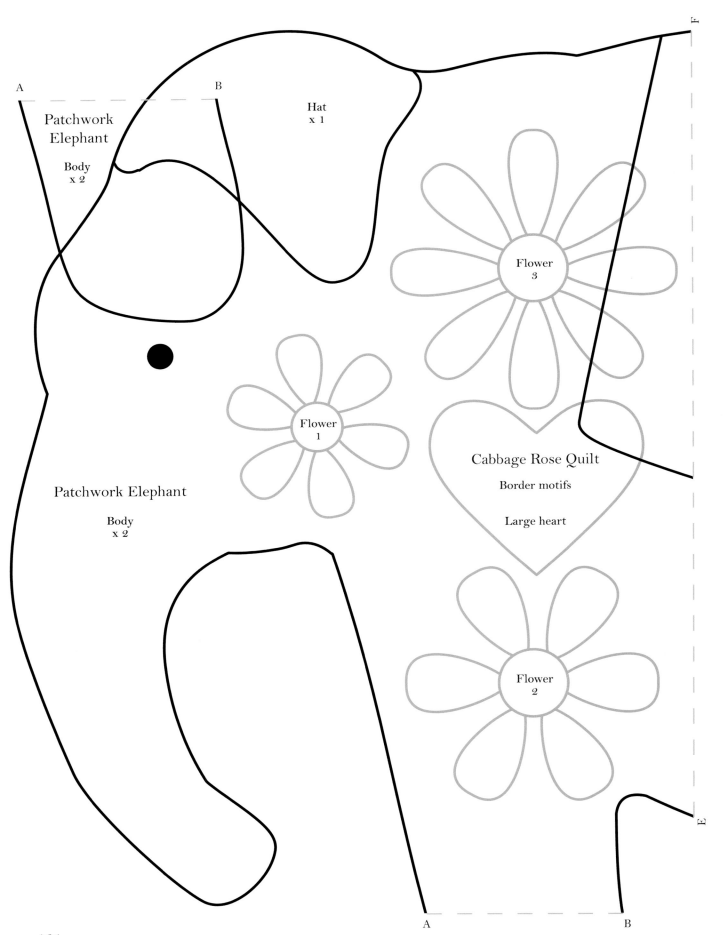

A

Patchwork
Elephant

Body
x 2

B

Hat
x 1

F

Flower
3

Patchwork Elephant

Body
x 2

Flower
1

Cabbage Rose Quilt

Border motifs

Large heart

Flower
2

E

A

B

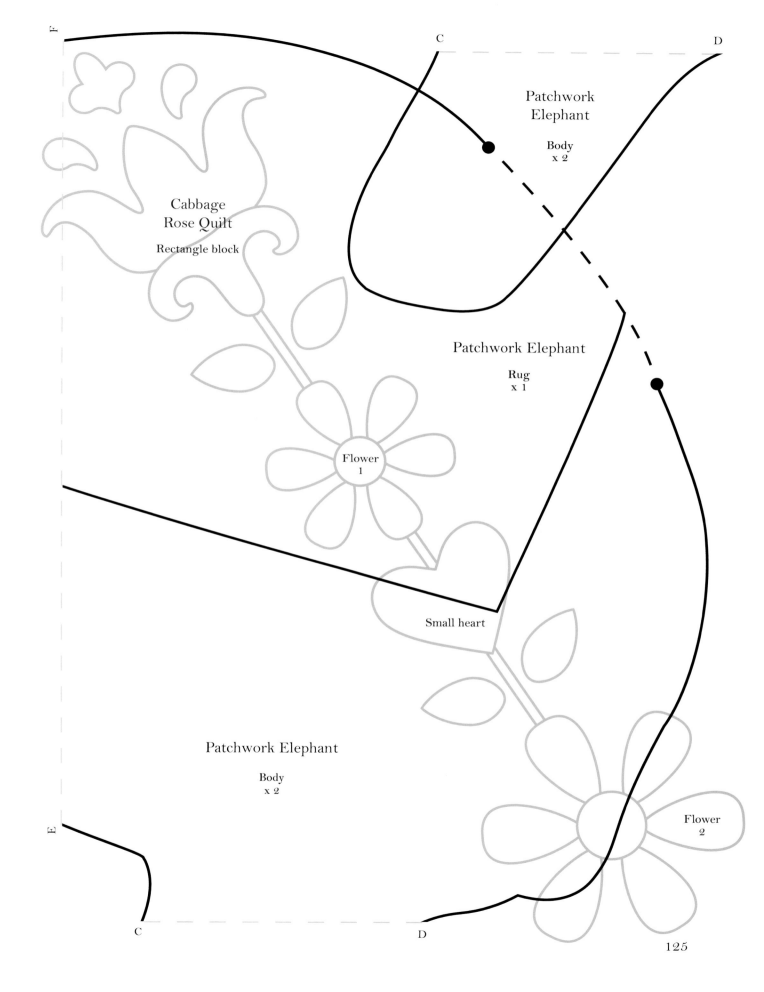

F

C

D

Patchwork
Elephant

Body
x 2

Cabbage
Rose Quilt

Rectangle block

Patchwork Elephant

Rug
x 1

Flower
1

Small heart

Patchwork Elephant

Body
x 2

Flower
2

E

C

D

Cabbage Rose Quilt

Square block

One half of the pattern.
Copy this and then reverse
(flip) the pattern to draw
the other half

Flower
1

Flower
3

Flower 2

Large heart (copy from Border motifs)

C

C

B

Patchwork Squirrel

Body
x 2

Label

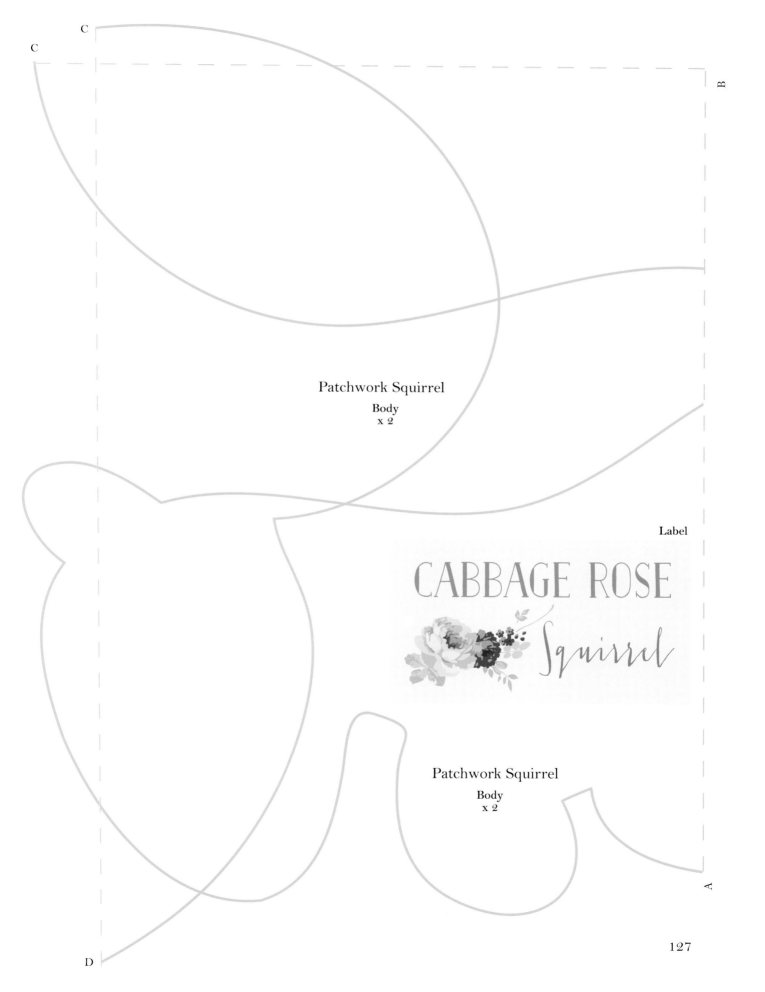

CABBAGE ROSE
Squirrel

Patchwork Squirrel

Body
x 2

A

D

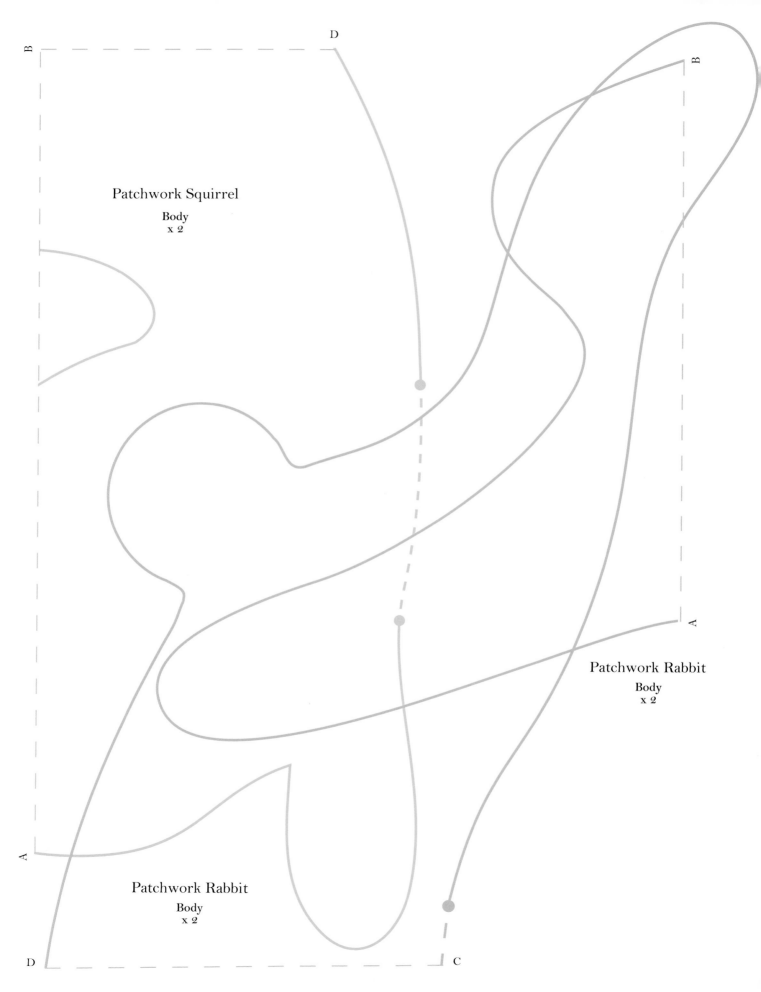

B

D

Patchwork Squirrel

Body
x 2

B

A

Patchwork Rabbit

Body
x 2

A

Patchwork Rabbit

Body
x 2

D

C

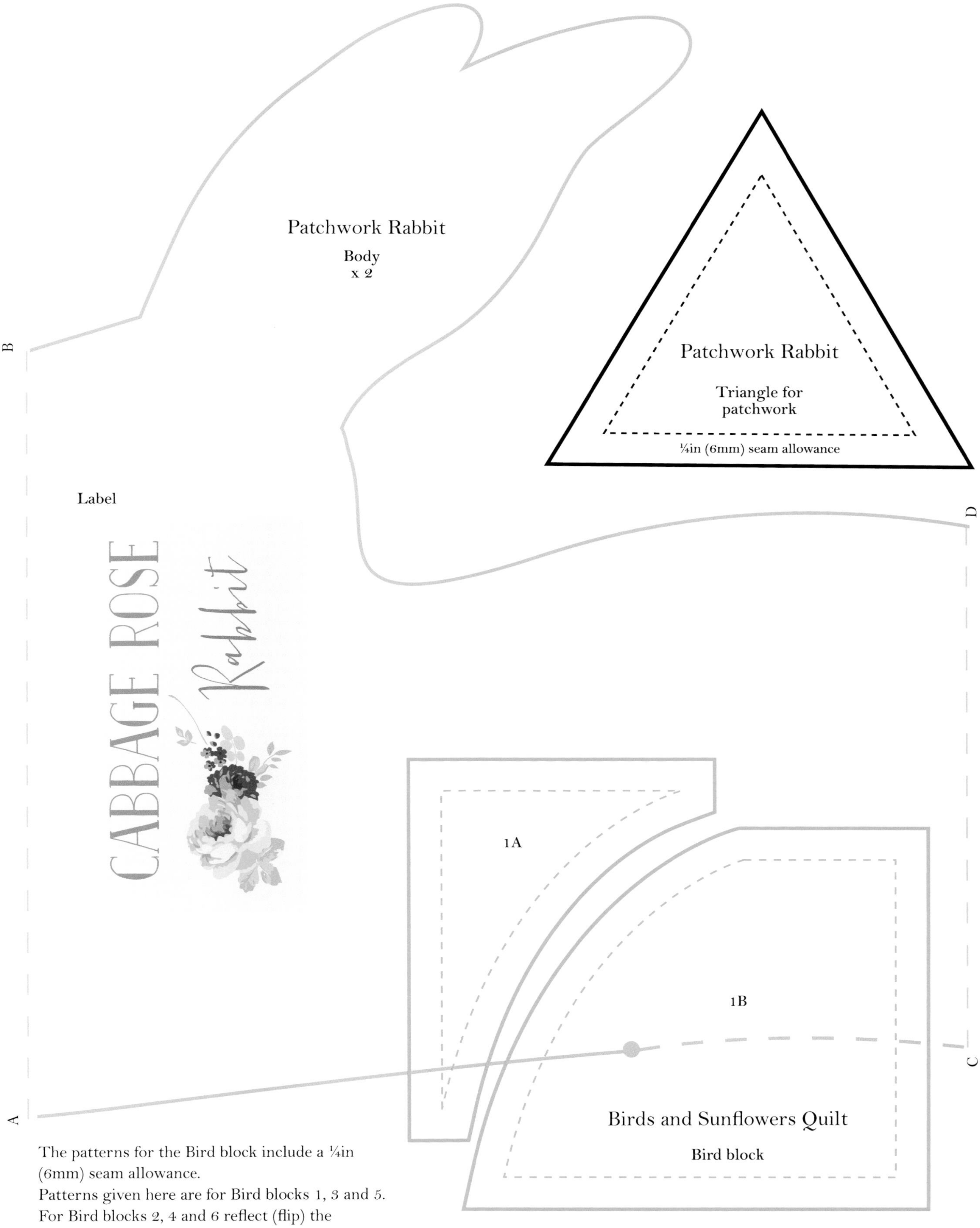

Patchwork Rabbit

Body
x 2

Label

CABBAGE ROSE

Rabbit

Patchwork Rabbit

Triangle for patchwork

¼in (6mm) seam allowance

B

D

A

C

1A

1B

Birds and Sunflowers Quilt

Bird block

The patterns for the Bird block include a ¼in (6mm) seam allowance.
Patterns given here are for Bird blocks 1, 3 and 5. For Bird blocks 2, 4 and 6 reflect (flip) the patterns before use.

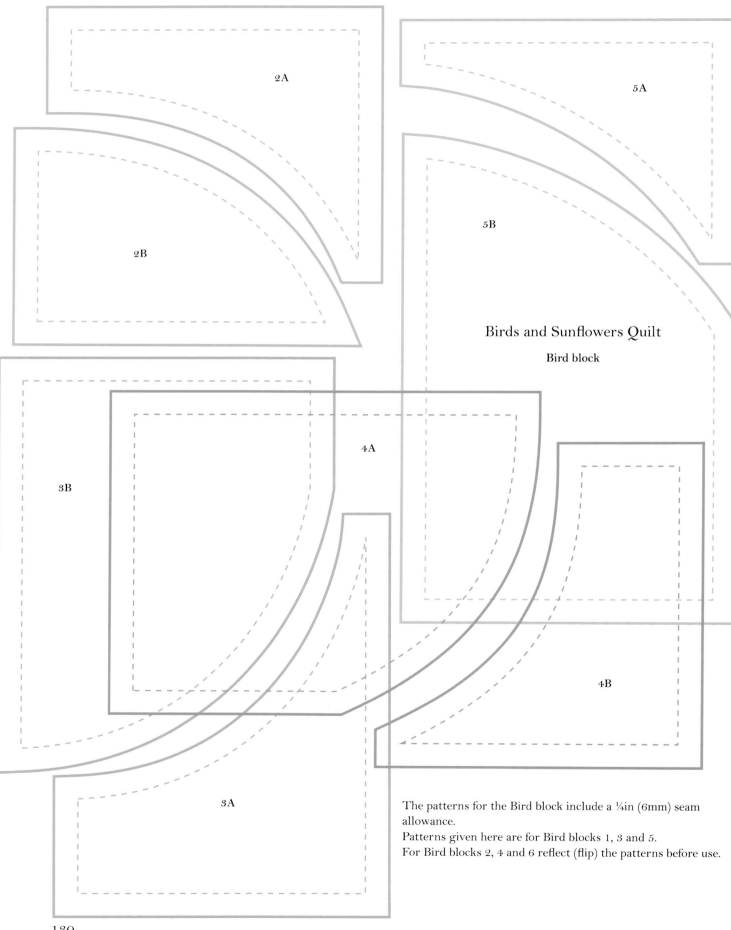

Birds and Sunflowers Quilt

Bird block

2A

2B

5A

5B

3B

4A

3A

4B

The patterns for the Bird block include a ¼in (6mm) seam allowance.

Patterns given here are for Bird blocks 1, 3 and 5.

For Bird blocks 2, 4 and 6 reflect (flip) the patterns before use.

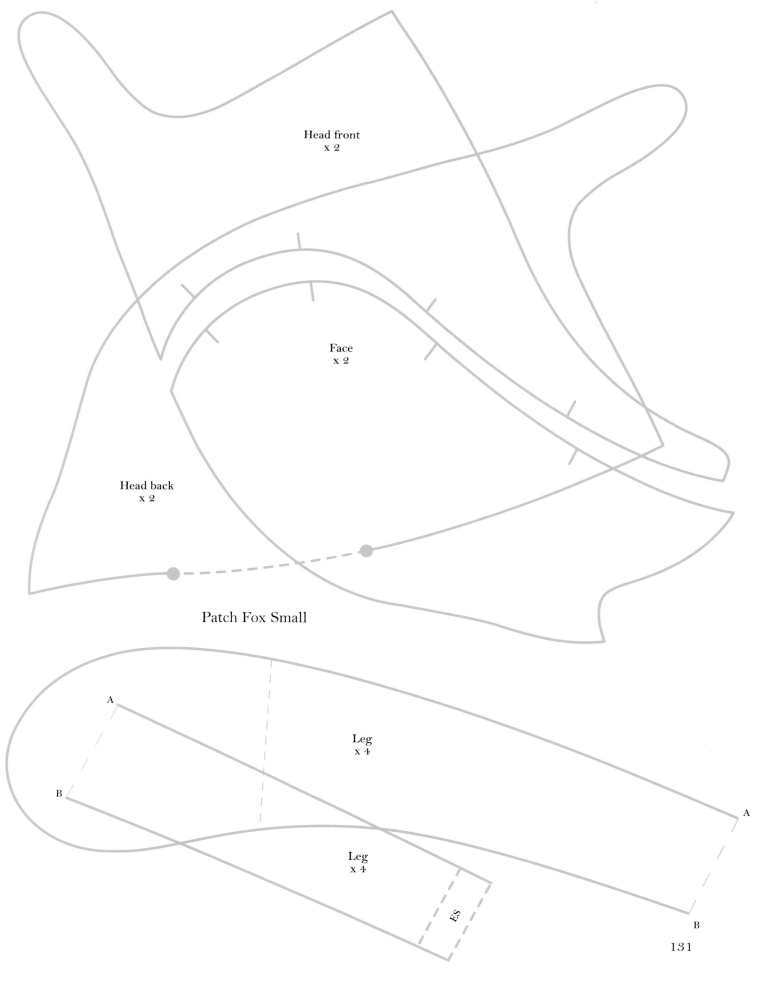

Head front
x 2

Face
x 2

Head back
x 2

Patch Fox Small

A

B

Leg
x 4

Leg
x 4

A

B

ES

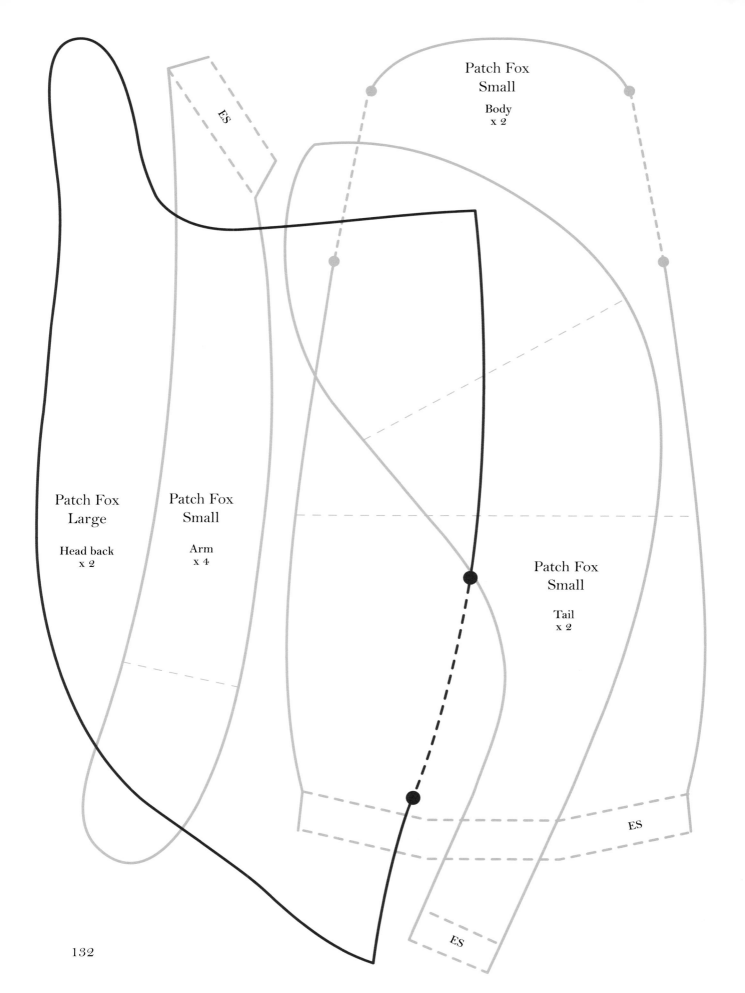

Patch Fox
Small

Body
x 2

ES

Patch Fox
Large

Head back
x 2

Patch Fox
Small

Arm
x 4

Patch Fox
Small

Tail
x 2

ES

ES

132

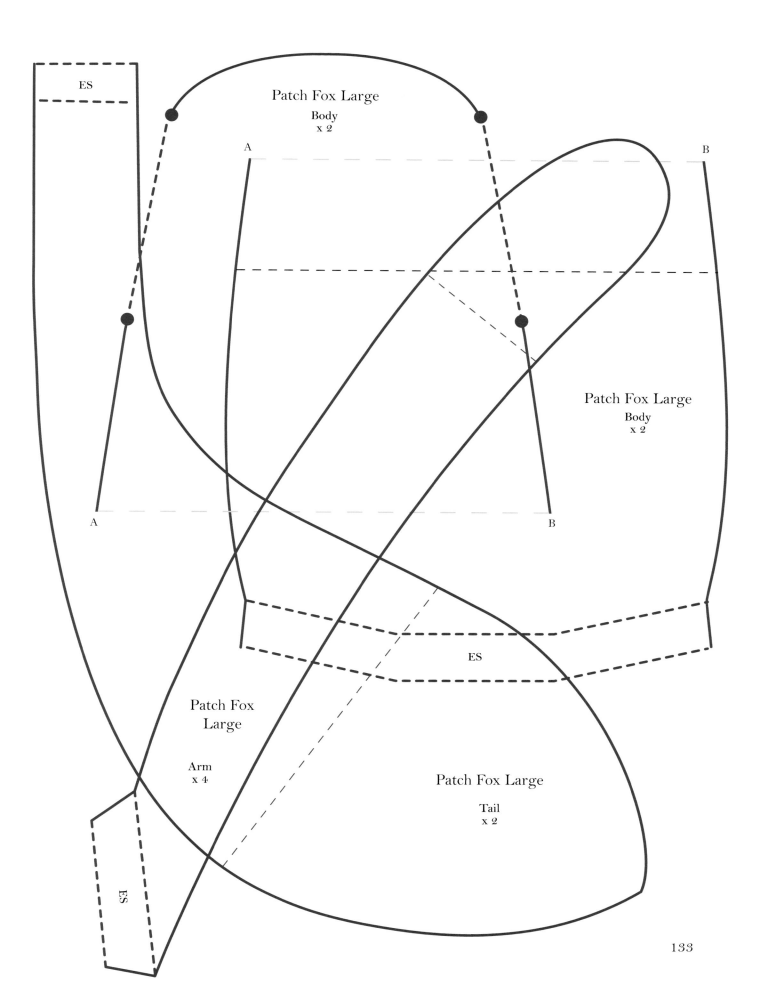

ES

Patch Fox Large
Body
x 2

A

B

A

B

Patch Fox Large
Body
x 2

ES

Patch Fox
Large

Arm
x 4

Patch Fox Large

Tail
x 2

ES

133

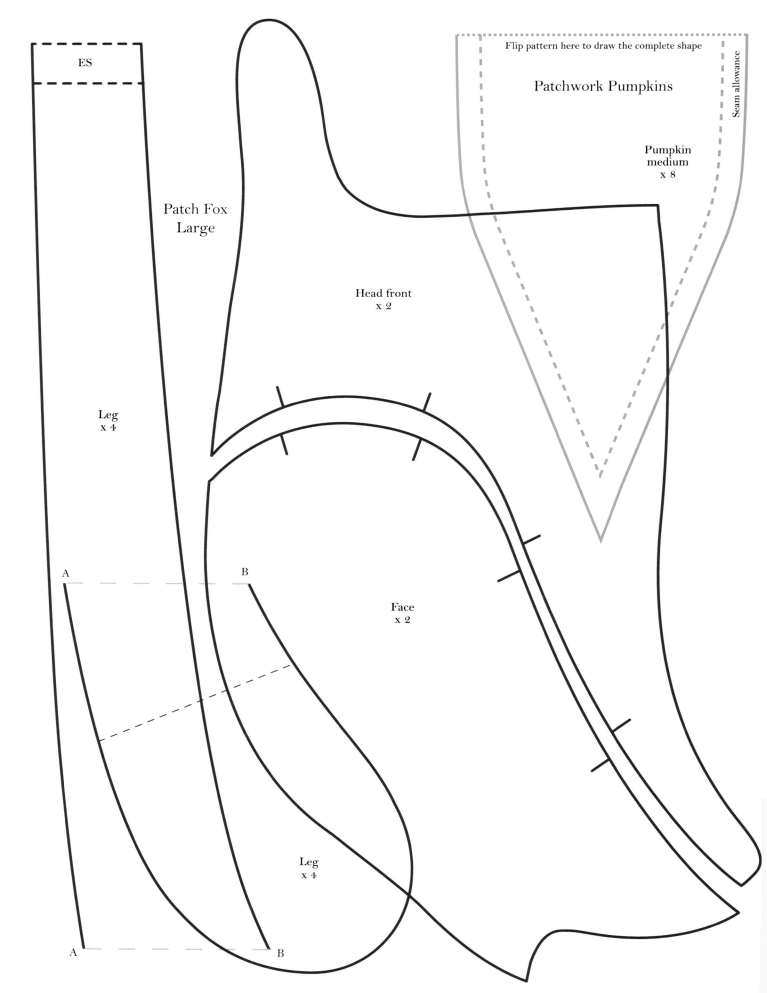

ES

Patch Fox
Large

Leg
x 4

Head front
x 2

A

B

Face
x 2

Leg
x 4

A

B

Flip pattern here to draw the complete shape

Patchwork Pumpkins

Pumpkin
medium
x 8

Seam allowance

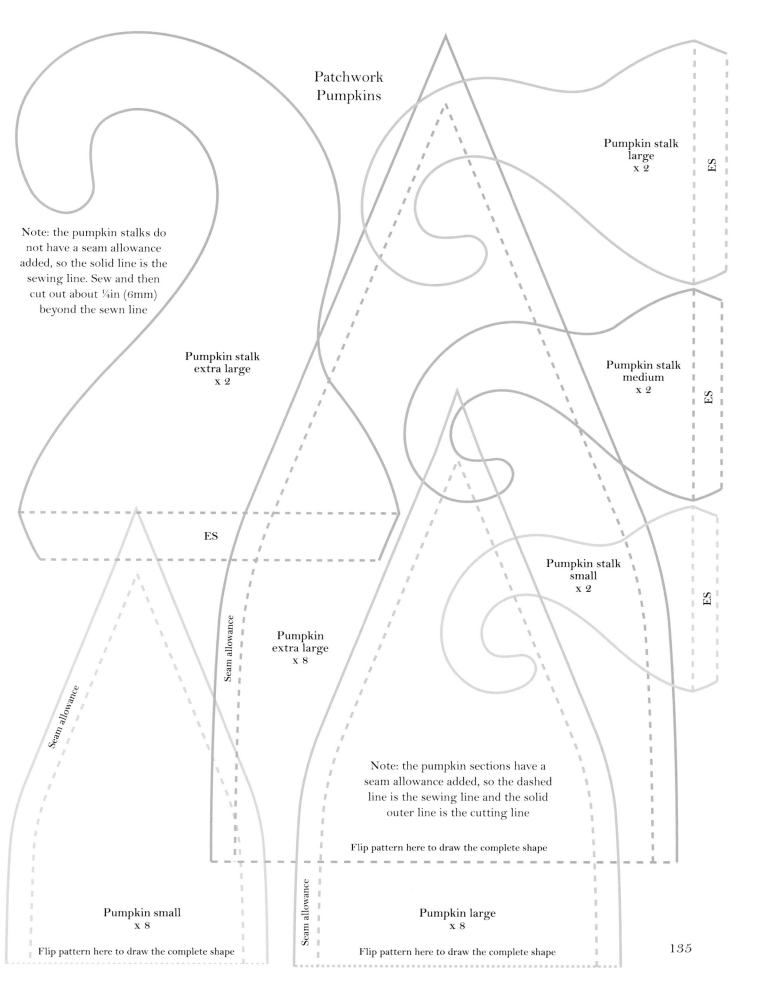

Patchwork
Pumpkins

Note: the pumpkin stalks do not have a seam allowance added, so the solid line is the sewing line. Sew and then cut out about ¼in (6mm) beyond the sewn line

Pumpkin stalk
large
x 2

ES

Pumpkin stalk
extra large
x 2

Pumpkin stalk
medium
x 2

ES

Pumpkin stalk
small
x 2

ES

Seam allowance

Pumpkin
extra large
x 8

Seam allowance

Note: the pumpkin sections have a seam allowance added, so the dashed line is the sewing line and the solid outer line is the cutting line

Flip pattern here to draw the complete shape

Seam allowance

Pumpkin small
x 8

Pumpkin large
x 8

Flip pattern here to draw the complete shape

Flip pattern here to draw the complete shape

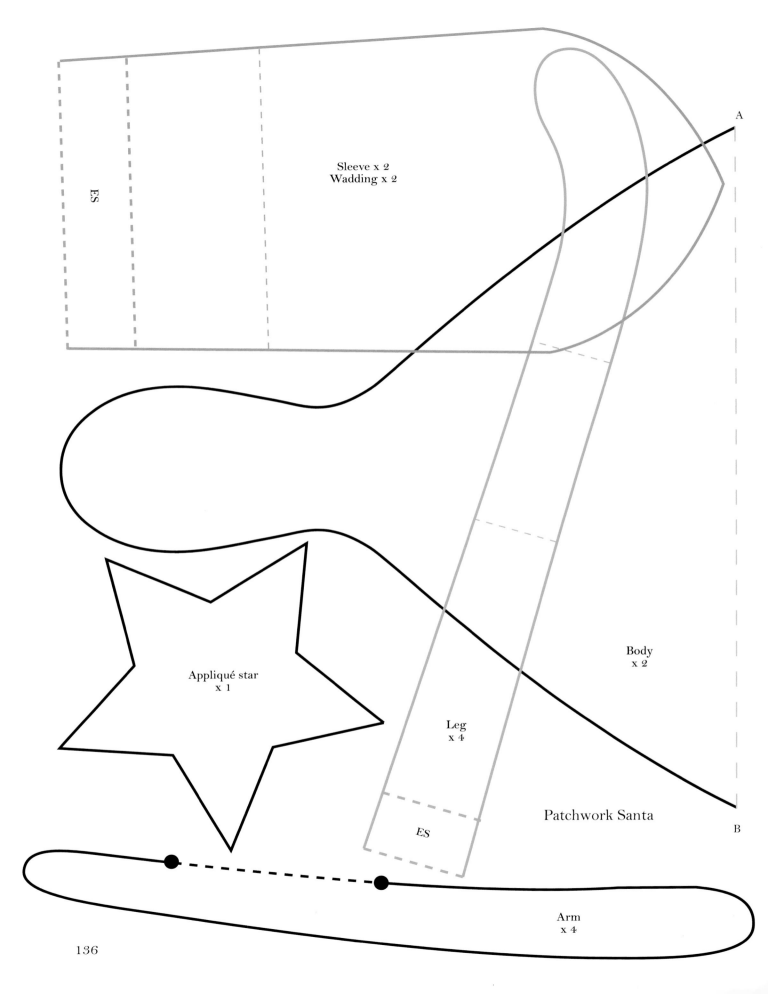

Sleeve x 2
Wadding x 2

ES

A

B

Body
x 2

Patchwork Santa

Appliqué star
x 1

Leg
x 4

ES

Arm
x 4

136

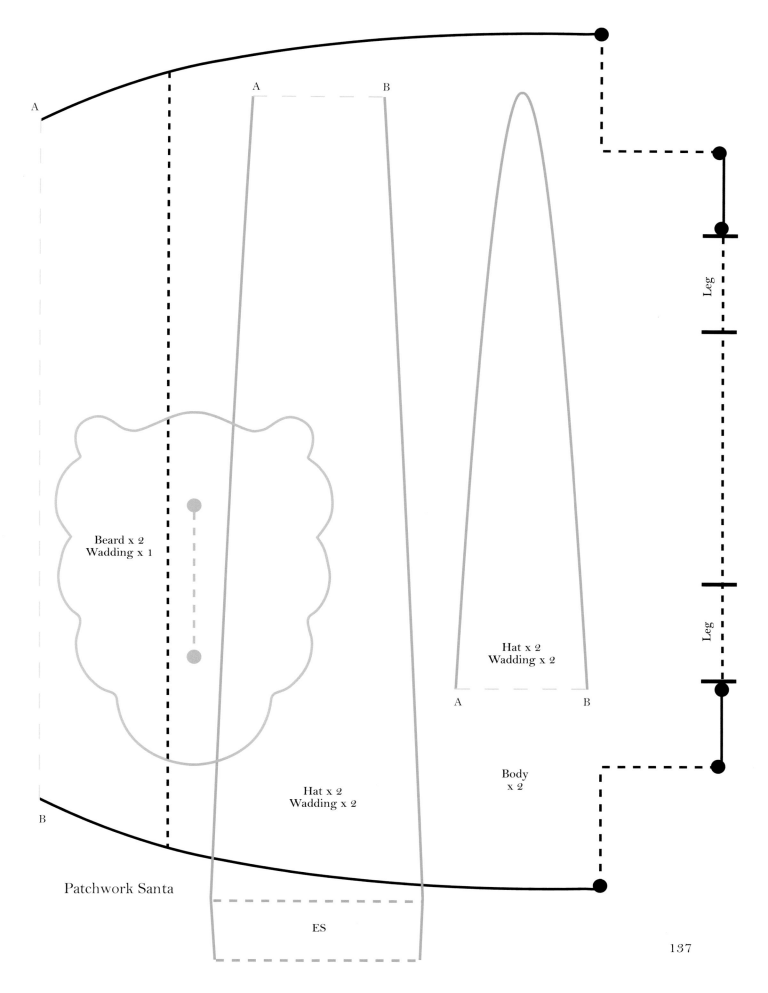

A

A   B

Leg

Beard x 2
Wadding x 1

Leg

Hat x 2
Wadding x 2

A   B

B

Body
x 2

Hat x 2
Wadding x 2

Patchwork Santa

ES

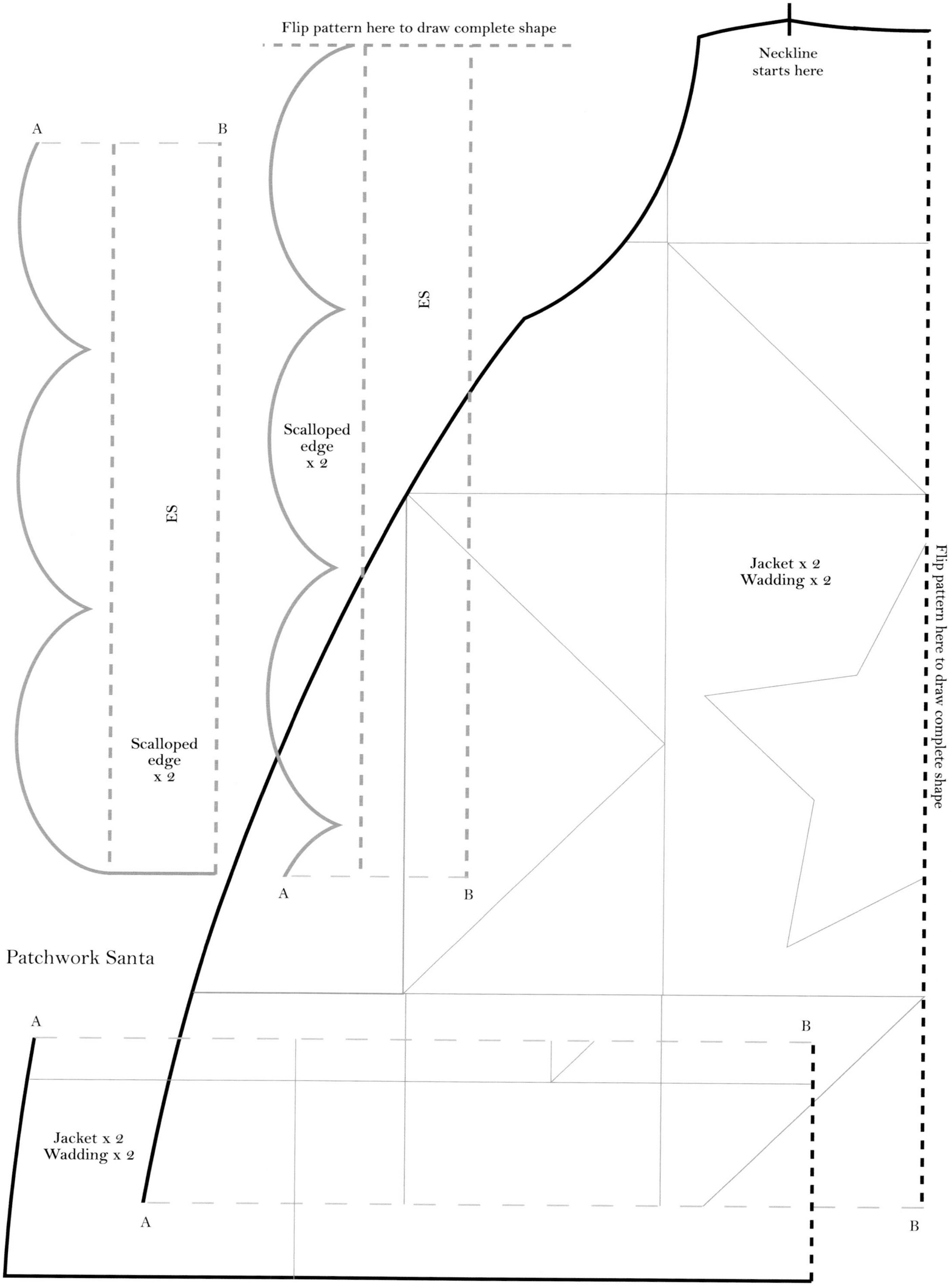

Flip pattern here to draw complete shape

A   B

ES

Neckline
starts here

A   B

ES

Scalloped
edge
x 2

Jacket x 2
Wadding x 2

Flip pattern here to draw complete shape

Scalloped
edge
x 2

A   B

Patchwork Santa

A   B

Jacket x 2
Wadding x 2

A   B

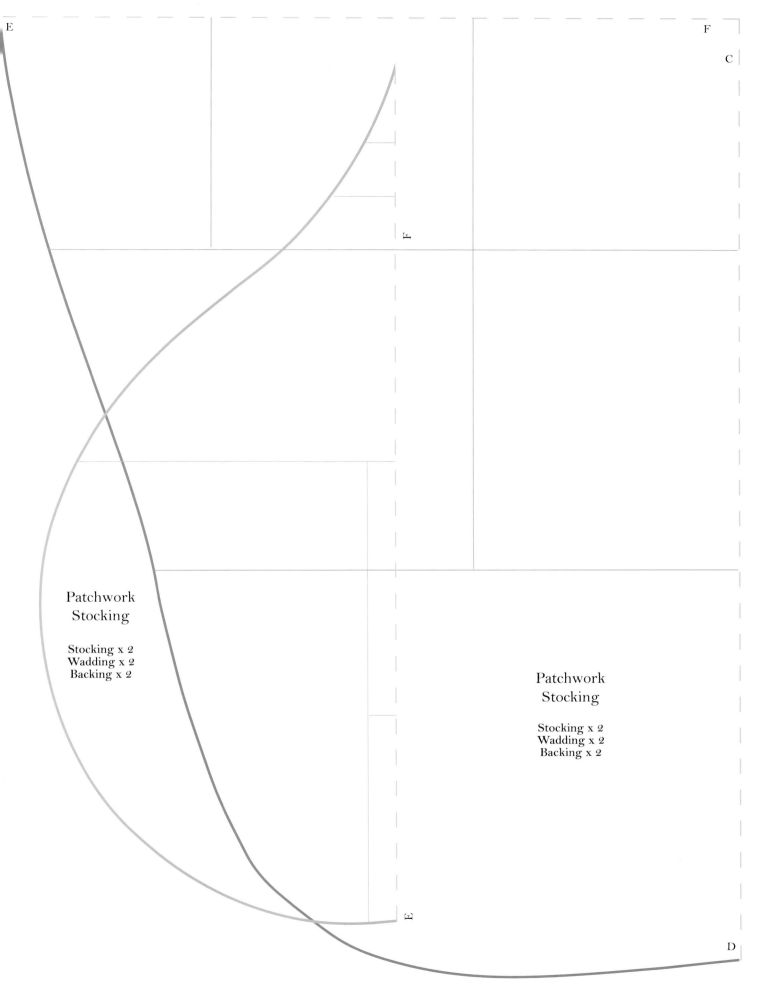

E

F

C

F

Patchwork
Stocking

Stocking x 2
Wadding x 2
Backing x 2

Patchwork
Stocking

Stocking x 2
Wadding x 2
Backing x 2

E

D

C

A

Patchwork
Stocking

Stocking x 2
Wadding x 2
Backing x 2

D

B

A

Use the Appliqué
Star pattern from
the Patchwork Santa
patterns

Patchwork
Stocking

Stocking x 2
Wadding x 2
Backing x 2

B

SUPPLIERS

Tilda fabric is stocked in many stores worldwide. To find your nearest Tilda retailer, please search online or contact the Tilda wholesaler in your territory. For more information visit: www.tildafabrics.com.

EUROPE

Marienhoffgarden (Spain, Portugal, Germany, Italy, Holland, Belgium, Austria, Luxembourg, Switzerland and Denmark)
Industrivej 39, 8550 Ryomgaard, Denmark
Tel: +45 86395515
Email: mail@marienhoff.dk
www.marienhoff.dk

Industrial Textiles (Sweden, Norway, Finland, Iceland, Greenland and Germany)
Engholm Parkvej 1, 3450 Allerød, Denmark
Tel: +45 48 17 20 55
Email: mail@indutex.dk
www.indutex.dk

Groves (UK)
Eastern Bypass, Thame, OX9 3FU, UK
Tel: +44 (0) 1844 258 080
Email: sales@groves-banks.com
www.grovesltd.co.uk

Panduro Hobby (France)
BP 500, 74305 Cluses Cedex, France
Tel: +33 04 50 91 26 45
Email: info@panduro.fr
www.tildafrance.com

J. Pujol Maq Conf S.A. (Spain and Portugal)
Pol. Ind. Les Pedreres, sector B, C/ Industria 5, 08390 Montgat, Barcelona, Spain
Tel: + 34 933 511 611
Email: jmpairo@jpujol.com
www.ideaspatch.com

NORTH AMERICA

Devonstone Square Inc. (USA)
19 West 34th St., Ste. 1018, New York, NY 10001, USA
Email: info@devonstonesquare.com
www.devonstonesquare.com

JN Harper (Canada and USA)
8335 Devonshire Road, Mont-Royal, Quebec H4P 2L1, Canada
Tel: +1 514 736 3000
Email: info@jnharper.com
www.jnharper.com

ASIA

Sing Mui Heng Ltd. (Singapore)
315 Outram Road, #05-09 Tan Boon Liat Building, Singapore 169074
Tel: +65 62219209
Email: enquiry@singmuiheng.com
www.smhcraft.com

Mianhexin Trading Co.,Ltd. (FlowerQuilt) (China Mainland)
Room 1001, New World Serviced Apartment, No.136, West Taige Road, Yixing City, Jiangsu Province, 214200 China
Tel: + 86 (510) 87926550
Email: flowerquilt@hotmail.com
www.flowerquilt.cn

Quilt Friends (Malaysia)
C-G-33, G/Floor Block Camilia, 10 Boulevard, Sprint Highway, Kayu Ara PJU6A, 47400 Petaling Jaya, Selangor D.E., Malaysia
Tel: +60 377 293 110
Email: quilt_friends@outlook.com
www.quiltfriends.net

THG International Ltd. (Thailand)
55/5-6 Soi Phaholyothin 11, Phaholyothin Rd., Samsen Nai, Phaya Thai, Bangkok 10400, Thailand

Scanjap Incorporated (Japan, Hong Kong, Indonesia and Thailand)
Chiyoda-ku, Kudan-minami 3-7-12, Kudan Tamagawa Bld. 3F, 102-0074 Tokyo, Japan
Tel: +81 3 6272 9451
Email: yk@scanjap.com
www.tildajapan.com

Long Teh Trading Co. Ltd. (Taiwan)
No. 71, Hebei W. St., Beitun District, Taichung City 40669, Taiwan
Tel: +886 4 2247 7711
Email: longteh.quilt@gmail.com
www.patchworklife.com.tw

M&S Solution (South Korea)
Gangnam B/D 7F, 217, Dosan-daero, Gangnam-gu, Seoul, South Korea
Tel: +82 (2) 3446 7650
Email: godsky0001@gmail.com

AUSTRALIA

Two Green Zebras (Australia and New Zealand)
PO BOX 530, Tewantin, Queensland 4565, Australia
Tel: +61 (0) 2 9553 7201
Email: sales@twogreenzebras.com
www.twogreenzebras.com

AFRICA

Barrosa Trading Trust (Liefielove) (South Africa)
9D Kogel Street, Middelburg, Mpumalanga 1050, South Africa
Tel: +27 (0) 847 575 177
Email: liefielove11@gmail.com
www.liefielove.co.za

INDEX

Printed in the UK by Severn for:
David and Charles, Ltd
Suite A, Tourism House, Pynes Hill, Exeter, EX2 5WS

10 9 8 7 6

Content Director: Ame Verso
Managing Editor: Jeni Hennah
Project Editor: Linda Clements
Designer: Prudence Rogers
Stylists: Line Dammen and Ingrid Skaansar
Photographers: Inger Marie Grini and Sølvi Dos Santos
Production Manager: Beverley Richardson

David and Charles publishes high-quality books on a wide range of
subjects. For more information visit: **www.davidandcharles.com**.

Layout of the digital edition of this book may vary depending
on reader hardware and display settings.